IN A QUIET LAND

JOHN O' DONOGHUE

In A Quiet Land

WITH A FOREWORD BY
Sean O'Faolain

 "We have made our art
of common things"
WILLIAM BUTLER YEATS

COWARD-McCANN, Inc.
NEW YORK

TO

Eoin O'Duffy and Patrick Walsh who lifted me out of the mire;
Moya Llewelyn Davies who taught me what I know;
William Butler Yeats who encouraged her in teaching me;
Peter O'Reilly who introduced us;
Sean O'Sullivan who helped with folklore;
My sister, and my brother's wife, whose vigorous opposition to
the idea of publication so spurred me on to write;
and
All those people, living or dead, who have directly or indirectly
helped me to make this book:
I respectfully inscribe its pages.

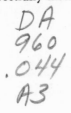

Foreword

I FIND this book most appealing because of its fresh innocence, its sense of wonder about the small, every-day things of life, whether in the routine of existence in the two-roomed cottage which the writer shares with his parents, sisters and brothers, or in Nature—flowers, streams, seasons, stars in the sky. What is so refreshing is that O'Donoghue seems to be seeing things with his own eyes for the first time, and speaks of them, their beauty or poignancy, with his own heart—not with self-conscious literary eyes or heart. The eye is unspoiled, it is clear; the heart has not been affected by second-hand experiences, so that though at first one may tremble a little at the seeming danger of sentimentality one is soon reassured—it is not sentimentality that one senses, it is sheer ingenuousness, kindness, natural delicacy of feeling using very simple language and simple images. The personality is unspoiled. It is all as if these ancient things had never happened before to anyone: as when his mother swings the pot of potatoes over the fire and "knuckles" the top ones down to make them level with the rest; or we see the birds and insects coming into the kitchen at night; or the trout swimming in the river like arrows. In the hands of a literary man these things might become "corny." Not with O'Donoghue.

This does not prevent him from being instinctively aware of and responsive to the presence of traditions, the sense of traditions, a fashioned way-of-life whose harshness is, he sub-consciously realises, softened by mutual love, by an inherited art—folk-lore, popular beliefs, an unelaborated poetry, all of which adds an element which we, outside that way-of-life, can recognise as folk-culture, so that while we partake in his instinctive pleasure we can also rationally appreciate the sources of it. For example, we can see that there is a certain cosiness in this way-of-life even while we are conscious of its harshness, but we can also see that it trembles on the edge of the fourth dimension—a notion which he would never express

5

but which his descriptions do force on us. So: when his grandmother dies he conveys not only the sorrow they feel, the love
for her that they always had, and the friendliness of the neighbours, but he also introduces, without any self-conscious fuss,
an eternal and timeless quality by mentioning such details as
that at the death one of the women stops the clock by taking a
hair-pin from her head to halt the pendulum; that for some
reason the lid of the coffin is laid to the left of the door and the
coffin itself to the right; that before the burial the nails of the
lid are loosened so that the final resurrection of the body
should not be delayed. In other words, the fourth dimension
is added unconsciously and the whole effect gains enormously
in authenticity thereby.

Such customs and beliefs, the very essence of folk culture
and the stuff of poetry, precious at all times are to-day becoming
rarer than gold. They cannot be fostered or cultivated, for that
would be to make them self-conscious and unreal, they can only
be observed and gratefully enjoyed where we are lucky to come
upon them woven into some such delightful autobiography as
In a Quiet Land.

SEAN O'FAOLAIN

Contents

I

My First Memories

WHEN the first hazy dawning of the fact that I existed came slowly in upon me I very foolishly thought that I was the centre of everything and that the world was there for my express convenience and delight. How could I have thought otherwise, and I after hearing soft voices around me on every side with an occasional "Whisht now, and don't wake Brian," whenever anyone spoke loudly in my presence?

If I had had any sense I should be able to see what a worthless creature I was and how thankful I should be for all the care I was getting, but I took everything for granted indeed and made the most of my position while it lasted.

The world as I first knew it was made up of four rough white-washed walls, a shiny-black loft and a floor of uneven flagstones. I was attracted by the bright light of the peat-fire that sparkled on the open hearth, but I was saved from it by the loving hands of older people who were always on the watch.

By degrees I began to see that there was something else beyond the four walls. Looking through the narrow doorway in the daytime I wondered at the great brown and blue mountains in the distance and at night I was delighted to see the lovely golden moon arising in the east. I wanted it taken down and given to me so that I might roll it about in my hands as I had seen my father do with the golden sovereigns he brought home from the fairs and markets. But my people told me they could not reach for it just then. Someone gave me a penny instead and that turned me from the path of lunacy for the time being.

When I was left out of the house at last I remember my mother taking me to a field in which my father was ploughing. I saw crows fly down to pick worms from the freshly-turned soil and I thought I might be able to catch them as I did the hens that fed from a dish in the yard. When I found my mistake

I asked my mother to catch one for me. She only laughed, for like the case of the moon, she was not able enough for the job, being rather heavy-footed, so I had to do without the crows. That was how I first learned that I could not have everything I wanted.

I never remember having any toys. My sisters, Bridget, a year older, and Eileen, a year younger than me, had to do without them also. In after years when my younger brothers became uneasy in the cradle I saw my mother knot a few straws in the shape of a bow-tie and hand it to them. They looked as pleased as if it had been a costly toy. Lack of toys was a good policy for the peace of the house, for no sooner did one child see another with something new than he or she wanted to have it and a row began for its possession.

At certain seasons very beautiful birds of a greyish-white colour would appear among the crows and I would be ten times more anxious to catch them because they were so rare. I wondered greatly why they would not let me do so for I meant to do them no harm. My father explained that they came from the western sea which lay far away beyond the deep blue hills and that they were gulls, not crows.

This valley in which I found myself longing for the moon, the crows and the seagulls was of great loveliness. It was like a big bowl with magnificent hills around it on all sides. When I looked at their glorious blue rim as the sun went down I wondered what was beyond them. If a person went over the rim I thought he would fall away into endless space. The great red sun too looked beautiful and full of mystery. Its slanting rays gave extra glory to the lovely valley. When it went down it left the sky above a rich red and gold in pleasing contrast to the peaks of indigo below. Looking at that sky and at these mountains through the clear fragrant air I thought the scene was surely a synopsis of all that was grand and glorious in the world. I was very happy with new hopes each day and loving relatives and friends about me speaking with a mixture of English and Irish to such an extent that I never knew where one tongue began or the other ended and I thought everyone in the whole world talked with the same melody and richness in their speech.

As I grew older and stronger I wandered about the farm

10

with Bridget and Eileen. We played housekeeping among the ruins of the little cabins left vacant after the great famine of long ago. We climbed into the crevasses among the rocks on the hills above. Every nook and corner has a host of memories for me but dearest of all are the thoughts of the little thatched cabin in which we lived. It was white-washed on the outside and there was a small window to the left and another to the right of the front door which had a crude and rattling latch. Strong laths were nailed outside the lower panes on the windows to protect them from the cows who sometimes ran against them when the gadflies attacked them in the summer. Above the door and windows hung the thick drooping eaves of the grey-brown thatch under which little birds came in the springtime to build their nests.

My grandmother is knitting a sock in the corner beside the fire, her needles flashing in the light and a sack-apron covering her blue flannel dress. A ball of thread is resting on her lap. When it falls and rolls away I pick it up and take it back to her. I am rewarded with a kiss and coaxing words of praise. "My love for you for ever, Brian, my little star of brightness," she says in Irish and adds in English: "I don't know in the world what I would do without you. May the Lord spare you the nimble sinews."

My mother is standing at the table which rests beneath the kitchen window. She is kneading a cake and humming a tune at the same time. She tightens the strings of her sack-apron as she moves towards the door and looks out, her mind wandering as she mutters something to herself. She stands at the door for a little while and rubs her brow with the back of her hand. As she does so I can see the dough sticking to her fingers. Then she goes back to the table while I watch the blazing peat and wonder at the mystery of fire. I look up at my green mug on the dresser beside Bridget's and Eileen's and at the woven old straw rope hanging by the wall from the ends of two beams and holding up a great number of socks. My grandfather had made it a few years before he died, God rest his soul. I am thinking what a clever man he must have been and I hardly notice the conversation of my elders until my thoughts are suddenly disturbed by a violent change in the usually gentle voice of my grandmother.

11

"Work that cake well with your hands, my girl," she said, addressing my mother in a rough tone of command, "and don't kill the lot of us with your badly-made flour-bread."

"Shut your mouth there in the corner," said my mother in a rage, for though she too was very gentle she had a terrible temper that sometimes came upon her like a clap of thunder, the Lord save us, "and mind your own business, you old cuilock. It was little flour you had in the house before my money came here to save you from the bailiffs."

My heart was up in my mouth for fear they might throw something at each other or begin to tear each other's hair and I could do nothing to stop them.

When she heard the noise my sister Eileen came in and began to cry but neither of the women seemed to notice her with the height of fury that was on them.

"Am breersa fain," said my grandmother, "we had full and plenty before ever we saw either you or your money, and it wasn't watching the tail of the mackerel we were either like you and your people were west in Annaweelogue."

My mother had come from a little fishing village of that name about forty miles away and I always thought the seagulls came from the same place.

"Full and plenty, indeed," said my mother, resuming her work at the cake, "and you have the signs of it on you to-day. I know very well what you had. Plenty porter and whiskey in Gurthagreenane whenever you went out, and yellow-meal gruel when you came back. A high life and dry bread is what you had, and that left you with this old poke-hole for a monument."

My mother always called our house an "old poke-hole" when she lost her temper with either my grandmother or my father.

During these rows each party threw as many slurs at the other as she could think of at the time and it was in that unpleasant way I learned a lot of our family history and background. When they had said everything they would run out of breath and stop as suddenly as they had begun. Both women seemed satisfied and the air was cleared. My sisters and I would get over the queer feeling of dread that had come upon us for our loved ones and by now we could hear again the crickets chirping in their hiding-places on the hob. I would stand close beside a great crack in the wall which was level with

12

my eyes and look in, but my grandmother would pull me back and warn me not to burn my clothes in the fire for I still wore petticoats like my sisters as is the custom with boys in our valley. Indeed I was nearly seven years old before I got my first pair of trousers and even then, upon my soul, it was lazy enough I was in getting into them!

After each row my mother and grandmother would not talk to each other for two or three days. During that time if it became necessary to convey spoken messages as when one of them would see a thieving cow steal into a field of growing corn and she could not turn the animal out herself because of minding the baby or some such job she would just say: "Eileen, girl, there is a cow in the corn. She must be put out." The other woman would then rush out to call my father who was better at managing cattle than anyone else about the place. Or maybe when my grandmother would turn her back on the nice piece of fresh beef she was preparing to cook, the cat would be in the act of pouncing on it when my mother would see him and shout: "Brian, my boy, look out for the cat," and my grandmother would know at once what he was after and remove the meat out of his reach. It is amusing how quick animals are to grasp their chance when the minds of people are taken up with serious problems. Our neighbour, Maura Nee Lhaera, a very jovial woman, was having her grandchildren gathered about her of a time saying the Family Rosary before going to bed. This is a very solemn ceremony and, apart from prayer, a strict silence must be observed. Maura was leading in grand style, saying the first half of each prayer in a loud voice while her grandchildren said the second. A few pig's feet lay on the table in front of them. The cat crept silently along underneath. "Pray for us, O Holy..." went on Maura with a weather-eye on Pussy, hoping for the best. Then: "Cat, you bastard, you!" she screamed as Pussy sprang on the table. "May the devil break your bones, and I cross you again, you bloody meddlesome scamp!" The prayers of course were ended in a loud laugh from all the others at the sudden change from a string of holy praises to a language only fit for thieves and vagabonds.

In the course of a week or so after each row my mother and grandmother would be friends again, and in the peace that followed, my grandmother would tell us fairy stories. The one I liked best was about a rich girl and a poor boy who fell in love. She told their story in order to teach us to keep our words if ever we gave them to anyone. The girl's father, she said, objected to the boy and, to separate them, he sent her a hundred miles away. But before she left she met her lover and he gave her his right hand and word that he would bring her back at a certain time before the year was out. This was an old Gaelic form of promise which was regarded as binding like an oath. Shortly after the girl left, however, the young man got sick and died. Nobody told the girl about him but as she was preparing to go to bed on the night appointed she heard his voice calling and asking her to come with him. She did not believe him at first until he showed her the hood he was carrying. It was her mother's. And the steed he had was her father's. He said he had come to take her home as he had promised to do. She got behind him on the horse which travelled faster than the wind. She kissed his lips, saying: "Mu veel a sthoir, you're as cold as clay," and he answered mournfully: "Oh, darling, my head is sore." On hearing this she tied a holland handkerchief about his head to ease the pain. When they came to her father's gate he told her to get down as it was growing late and the cock would soon be crowing. He advised her to go to bed and that he would look after the steed and have him fed in the stable. All the time she never knew that she had travelled a hundred miles with a dead boy! When she knocked at the hall-door her father answered. She asked if he had sent for her and he said he had not. She told him her lover had brought her back. On hearing this her father began to tear his hair in trouble for he knew that the young man was dead.

> "He wrung his hands and he cried full sore,
> And the young man's darling cried more and more."

The story was told in verses which my grandmother sang to a lonesome air. It went on to tell how they dug the young man's grave on the following morning and though he had been buried for nine months they found the holland handkerchief around his head.

I believed every word of the story because in our house there was always the height of respect for the dead and their power

14

of moving about when they wished. Sometimes I would dream of the fairies coming to me and then I would wake up in great fright. When the bite of an insect, perhaps a flea, made a small black mark on my shinbone my grandmother told me it was caused by a "fairy pinch," given when they came to poke fun at us. Our house, like most of its kind, had lots of fleas in it. It was very hard to get rid of them. Some said they came from the peat, others from the thatch. One of them would pinch my wrist and suck my blood to his heart's content while I kept an eye on him, thinking of the cruel death I would give him as soon as I was ready to lay my hand upon him. But by the time my hand was within an inch of his cursed body he was off in a mighty jump into a fold of my petticoat to return again perhaps when I was asleep and leave me like a dotted salmon putting blame upon an honest fairy for the damage!

Lice too were plentiful about the place but they were easy to catch. A "boody" was the nickname for a louse and he was the cause of many jokes. People were very sensitive about his presence and if he appeared on a man in public it was thought to be a great disgrace. The man would be called a "lousy bastard" behind his back.

Pat Mulloy, a neighbour of ours, used to say that a flea was a grandmother every twenty-four hours and as far as I could see the "boodies" lost no time either.

The women were always trying to get rid of these pests. They were afraid to have visitors on their account because if there was only one pet flea or one ailing boody in the house he was sure to make himself known to the stranger. When the visitor scratched the injured spot the woman of the house would say: "The devil carry that old culaun of a dog; he's ate alive with fleas," and she would draw an unmerciful kick at the poor unoffending animal lying quietly beside the fire. It was the same when a nasty smell came from the human body. Blame the dog, open the door, order him out, give him the toe of the boot and make him the scapegoat!

II

The Little House of Happiness

OUR house which was very small and cosy was built on the slope of a grey rock forming part of the Coomlaegill Mountain. It was thatched with straw. The kitchen was separated from the bedroom by a rough partition of unrabbeted lime-washed boards on one side and a big dresser on the other. Between these was "the room door" which was fastened by means of an iron hasp made by one of the local blacksmiths. The outer doors, front and back, were secured at night with wooden bolts instead of locks.

A low table stood under the light of the one small window in the kitchen. Long years of wear had taken off about six inches from its legs so that the cross-rails at the bottom nearly touched the ground. In one of its unrabbeted boards there was a black hollow caused by a candle having burnt itself out and into this my father was fond of putting the scrapings from his pipe while he prepared a new filling with a lot of ceremony. I remember every detail of that old table which is dearer far to my memory than a throne of gold would be in any other place.

On the opposite side of the kitchen stood "The Sate," a long settle with a high panelled back and strong arm-rests. It was made during the great famine, my grandmother said, by a carpenter called Thigue O'Carroll, a man who always used wooden pegs instead of nails, and by the same token it is as firm to-day as when he drove the last peg into it. A great knot in the back was always in front of my eyes when I knelt to say my prayers morning and evening as my grandmother had directed. The memory of that old knot is firmly fixed on my mind. An old bracket table rested on the settle and was always taken down for meals.

Between the settle and the back door stood "Nanny's Coop" in which my grandmother kept her hens while my mother kept hers in another standing against the partition already mentioned. These hens were the cause of much trouble when they got mixed up and laid their eggs in the wrong coops making the women have rows about them. My mother usually gave way to my grandmother on account of her age and the suspicion that she might be doting. Poverty made it necessary to keep hens in the kitchen on account of the shortage of out-houses.

We all slept together in the one room at first, my sisters and I with my grandmother in one bed and the younger children in another with my parents. The clay floor of this room was always damp. So were the walls. The bed-clothes had to be dried at the fire now and again. To save our feet from the floor my father made woven straw mats, putting one in front of each bed. A small window with a fixed sash let in the light. An old dresser with only one shelf at the top stood at the foot of my grandmother's bed which had a canopy over it. Under the seat of this old dresser was a big wooden chest which we called "Nanny's Box." We thought it was full of wonderful things. They were only shown on rare occasions and consisted of an Italian iron, a high-caul cap, a brown habit in readiness for her wake and funeral, a small green and yellow plaid shawl and a few other common articles, simple in themselves, but full of strange romance to our young minds. An oblong table stood against the southern wall or gable, opposite the room-door, and over it a mantelshelf, but there was no fireplace. On the shelf rested the coloured picture of a dead girl with angels watching over her. On each side of this were pictures of my father's and mother's people. To the left of the mantelshelf hung an orange-box on pegs. This was decorated with brightly-coloured wall-paper and was used for keeping ware and other things. Sacks of Indian meal were stored in the corner south of my parents' bed and rested on some limbs of ash to keep them off the floor. Everything was extremely simple and there was very little room left in which to move about.

The loft over the kitchen and bedroom was all in one. It was an awful gloomy-looking place getting only a little light from one tiny pane of glass in the southern gable and even that was partly hidden by the tall end of a wooden bed standing in front of it. Light also came up through the opening from the kitchen where a little wooden step-ladder stood. When I ventured up the steps to peep into the gloom the older people shouted at me to come down before I fell. I thought they also

17

wanted to save me from the pookies hiding above until the night came when they could come down, sit by the fireside, talk about old times, smoke their pipes or make themselves a saucepan of tea. They were always welcome to do so because they were our own pookies but I was anxious to be in bed before they came just the same. Hearing so much about them it was no wonder that they seemed as natural as the people I saw about me every day. As far as I could gather, each person became a pookee as soon as he or she had drawn the last breath, and wandered about at night when they had nothing else to do. Often I lay awake looking fearfully through the little window for the big pookee or "boody-man" my grandmother said would come for me if I did not do what I was told.

When I grew older I was put to sleep in the loft with my brother Murty. None of us liked the idea on account of our dread of the pookies but we had to be satisfied. Our parents' only dread was that we might fall through the unguarded opening where the ladder stood. Opposite our bed were my mother's two American trunks, black and shiny from the smoke which stole into every corner of the loft. She always warned us not to open any of them and this gave us the impression that they were full of great treasures. If my grandmother had wonders in her box my mother's trunks must be like The Valley of Diamonds. When we finally broke the rules and peeped in, we saw by the dim light a beautiful album with a green velvet cover containing pictures of her friends in America wearing old-fashioned dresses with balloon sleeves on their blouses and their hair cut short across their foreheads in a style which my father called the "Pony Fringe." With this album was a big thick book with beautiful pictures of Christ's Passion in lovely colours. There was my mother's gold watch and her wedding ring with many other treasures. Once I asked her why she was so strict about these trunks. "They have very heavy covers with sharp edges like knives," she said, "and I am always afraid they may fall suddenly and cut off your fingers." It was a big surprise for me to learn this because I always thought it was the treasures she was so careful about.

I remember the peace of that bed in the loft and how soundly I slept in it. When I woke in the morning I could see the cross-beams holding the rafters together. How Murty and I enjoyed

18

swinging from them and tossing each other about on the bed when we got down! Covering the rafters and rough làths pegged to them were long smoky strips of peat called "scrahs" to which the thatch was fastened by means of sally rods shaped like hairpins, the pointed ends of which could be seen sticking through inside, making the roof look like a great hackling machine. From end to end of the loft hundreds of spiders had hung their webs in all directions.

In spite of its gloom there was no superstition attached to the loft. It was uncanny enough without one, indeed. The part over the kitchen was used for storing potatoes in the winter. The boards were not rabbeted, so the dust would fall between them and sometimes run down inside my shirt when my mother disturbed them on going up with a lighted candle for a bucket of potatoes. The joists were rough unplaned tree trunks trimmed a little with an adze. They were black from smoke. The boards lying on them went down and up as weights on them were laid or lifted.

We were lucky that the kitchen was dry and cosy. Though the house was quaint in every respect it had a peculiar air of homely comfort about it which made it like a bird's nest. We were all very happy in it, thank God. I should never forget it if I lived in gilded mansions for a thousand years.

My mother and grandmother could talk in Gaelic. They usually did so when they did not want us to know what they were talking about. They had both been punished for using it in school when they were young so they decided on bringing us up to talk English lest we should find the world awkward later on if we only knew Gaelic. They were always mixing up the two languages so that for a long time we did not know which was which.

When my grandmother was not telling stories my mother would sing as she sat near the fire waiting for a pot or kettle to boil. She usually sang the sorrowful songs of Ireland in Gaelic and one of her favourite verses in that language said:

> "Little Colleen of the wild green rushes,
> There is trouble on the Clan Na Ghaeul."

Sometimes she would tell us about the beautiful singers she had heard in America, entirely different, she said, from those of Coomlaegill. She remembered one Irishman who sang on the stage and she would stand up to show us how he did it. Swaying her body to and fro she would sing as he did:

"Erin, my home, though from thee I roam,
My blessing I leave on your shore,"

going on to tell how he finished by sprinkling dust on the stage and singing:

"A handful of earth from the place of my birth
To the grave where my poor mother lies."

My father played heavenly music on the fife. He often did so on the winter nights. He rinsed out the fife with water before playing and when he started we all went into raptures. I have never heard anyone else play with the same plaintive, beautiful and appealing melody. So it will be seen that though we lived far out upon the mountains we always had plenty of amusement. My father kept his fife in a black box on the canopy of my grandmother's bed. We always said "Below in the room" because the house was built on a slope and the bedroom was lower than the kitchen. The whole townland was on the slope of a hill so we always said "above" and "below" instead of north and south. My grandmother was very careful about her bed which had belonged to her father. She told us that he kept his sword on top of it in the old troubled times. She had the canopy covered with wallpaper both inside and outside. This paper had designs of big red roses and green leaves on it. A picture of the Holy Family hung on the inside for the sleepers to see as they said their prayers. When I had to stay in bed with the measles and other sickness I remember examining all the details of that picture which had the walls of a town in the background. St Joseph had a beard and wore a long brown mantle. The Blessed Virgin wore a blue dress and a red mantle. The Holy Child was dressed in white. All three had bare feet. That seemed natural to us children who never wore boots or shoes of any kind. We were much lighter and happier without them. While waiting for leave to get up I traced the designs of the roses and leaves on the wallpaper as my eyes wandered from one to another. Sometimes I thought they were shaped like men, sometimes animals, whiskey bottles, the face of Paddy

20

Don't Care, our neighbour, with his black felt hat squeezed up like the folds of a concertina and lying rakishly on his head, or Pat Mulloy with his cap in the same way.

My grandmother would allow nobody to move her bed on any account, not even for cleaning. It was unlucky, she said, to move an old bed. So it always stood in the same position and I often wondered about the many curious things which had belonged to my aunts and uncles and which must have fallen between it and the wall. They must still be there, I thought, so I often climbed to the top by way of the old dresser and looked into the dark space between but I could see nothing for there was no window in that side of the room.

Wallpaper with bright red flowery designs also covered the loft-boards and the thick unplaned joists which held them up. Into some of these joists were driven old-fashioned pegs on which hung most of the older people's clothes.

On the outside the gable walls were built about a foot higher than the level of the scrahs so as to protect the verges from the wind. House-leek was always kept growing on top of these walls for it is believed that while it grows there the house will never be burned. My father warned us not to make fires in the yard for fear the sparks might fall on the thatch and set it alight.

When the little birds came to live with us in the spring and built their nests under the eaves my father told us not to put our hands into the nests. If we did, he said, the birds would forsake them, and there was also the danger of our hands getting paralysed for having interfered with them. But in spite of everything we often offended in this respect with regard to our little feathered visitors.

On the dawning of a May morning when the trees are greening and the corn rising, thousands of birds fill up the fragrant air of the valley with rich and glorious melody.

We had visits also from other creatures as well as the birds. In damp weather snails would find their way into the kitchen at night and be found hiding in corners when the daylight came. Earwigs too were plentiful in the house and so were beetles. One little creature had a superstition attached to him. He only appeared now and again and travelled fairly fast, keeping the hind part of his body up in the air in an amusing fashion. He was called "The Dhoradhaeul." He was shown no mercy as he was supposed to represent the devil and whenever he appeared the cry went out: "Kill the Dhoradhaeul! Blast you, kill the bastard!" Why should he always be killed, I asked, when he was doing no harm? He raised his tail at the trial of our Lord, I was told, and shouted: "Crucify Him! Crucify Him!" for it was the devil himself who took that shape at the time!

III

The Fairies

THE Pookies were sometimes called "The Good People" and the information we got about them did not come in the usual form of fairy tales but from the everyday talk of the people.

Whenever any of the neighbours came in we were full of excitement as well as being eager to listen and learn.

Maura Nee Lhaera comes slowly down the rock above the house with careful steps, a strong hazel stick in her hand, a bright check apron covering her blue flannel dress and red petticoat, a cheerful smile on her fat round face and a generous heart in her bosom.

"Lie down, Shep," shouts my mother, "lie down, you old culaun," for the dog is barking loudly at the feet of Maura.

"He won't touch me, indeed," says Maura, "for he knows me well. He's making a foolish fuss, that's all."

"He knows you're welcome anyhow," says my mother as Maura reaches the yard and stands to admire two fat pigs lying in the litter beside the fence.

"God Almighty bless them," says Maura, "before I'd overlook them, Annie. Haven't you two fine pigs!" and she throws a spit on them to keep away the evil spirits.

"They're not too bad," says my mother, walking towards them. "We're hoping to have them for the next fair with God's help."

"Upon my soul, then, they're no shame to you," says Maura, poking them with her stick to make them rise so that she may have a better look at them, "and you should make a nice penny on them if I know anything about fat kaishes."

The pigs grunt in protest as they stand up and poke their noses into the litter.

"They'll help to pay the rent for us anyhow," says my mother as they both come towards the door.

"Glory be to the Lord God, Maura," says my grandmother,

"isn't it well you can travel, and I suppose you must be shoving up to sixty years if you're a day old for they say Den O'Grady west here and yourself are the one age."

"The one age then surely, Joan," says Maura, sitting on the settle, her face beaming all the time as if everything in the world pleased her as well as fat pigs, "and 'tis telling on me too. God knows 'tis time for me now to get tired on the feet for 'tis many a long day since I first came to Coomlaegill. Himself above here is five years older nor me and he was born in The Year of the Big Snow. That will tell you without going to the book that none of us are chickens now, indeed."

Nobody living on the farms of the parish of Gurthagreenane ever kept an account of the years according to the calendar. They always referred to the past as "The Night of the Big Wind; The Year of the Big Flood; The Night Father Mack died; The Day Paddy the Pimples broke his leg"; and so on.

"How are all the young O'Shannisseys?" Maura enquires as we gather about her staring with our mouths open.

"A fright to the world out for devilment, then," says my mother as she and my grandmother try to put a stop to our childish curiosity and impudence, going on to tell her of the many scrapes we had got into for the past few days, suggesting here and there in Gaelic the remedies which might prevent the same things happening again. Talking about these things soon leads to thoughts of what happened to older people in the past and it is now we gather closer to Maura as she tells her wonderful tales.

"Annie, you didn't know my father, God rest his soul," she begins, settling herself back on the settle as my mother sits opposite her on a little black stool and prepares to darn a sock while my grandmother adds a few sods of peat to the fire after having brushed the ashes aside with a heather broom.

"I did not then, indeed, Maura, but I often heard tell of him."

"Im breersa fain, you did, I suppose. Ouliveen Rue they called him. He was a well-known man in his day and a great hand at the scythe or any other article a farming man could use."

"He was all that, indeed," says my grandmother, joining in

24

the talk as she sat on a creaking chair between the two. "I knew him well, and all belonging to him, God rest their souls."

"Amen a Heirna," says Maura with a deep sigh. "You did, of course, woman dear. Why shouldn't you and he living in the next townland to your old home at Bohereenfhadda."

"That's true for you, and you may be sure that he was the good obliging neighbour, may God reward him for it."

"Amen," says Maura again and she went on: "But to return to my story, why. He was out of a day mowing hay for his cousin Murty the Dogs and it was late that night when he was coming home with the scythe over his shoulder, for Murty kept him there playing cards till the small hours and they never felt the time passing."

"They didn't, of course," says my grandmother, "for the devil is always following the pack, the Cross of Christ between us and the dirty beast. They say he's under the table whenever a game is played."

When I hear this I say in my own mind that he must be like our dog who is fond of lying under the table or settle at all times, game or no game.

"You know the steps across the fence by the side of the road below my father's place," says Maura.

"I do, indeed," says my grandmother, "for it was many a time I passed them on my way to Killarney."

"Well, by the same token, he was just in the act of putting his foot on the bottom step when, the Lord between us and all harm, didn't he see the woman standing before him at the top!"

"God guide and guard us!"

"He stepped back to let her pass like any man would do, but faith and sure, the devil a move did my lassie make any more nor the stone she was standing on. He stepped up then, thinking she might be going towards the house with him but there she stayed like a brazen statue with a vicious look on her face. It suddenly struck my father then that she might be from the other world, the Lord save us. He was beginning to lose courage till with the will of God he thought of the scythe."

"Yes, then, Maura," puts in my mother, "they say the scythe or anything made of steel is a great protection against the fairies."

"It is, to be sure," says Maura, "or a hazel stick like that,"

25

holding up the one she carries. "Well and good, why, my father stepped up to her and says he: 'Leave my way, in the Name of God.' Eroo, with that she made a drive towards him and if she did why he drew the scythe at her. The Lord save us, she let a screech out of her that would wake the saints in glory. The scytheboard fell to the ground and she stamped on it. When my father stooped to pick it up didn't his hand get suddenly paralysed, God save the mark, and the spirit disappeared. When he got home he was as white as a sheet and as weak as a chicken."

"Small blame to the poor man," says my grandmother, waving her hands at a hen that has taken advantage of the quietness to steal in and help herself through a hole in a sack of meal near the door and then flies off in fright as Maura continues:

"They put him to bed, of course, and he was lying there for many a long day on the flat of his back with no hope of recovery until they thought of sending for Father O'Leary, God rest him, and telling him the whole story. Father James was the boy for cases like that. He looked at the patient and, shaking his head, says he: 'You got a bad stroke, man dear,' says he, 'and you're lucky to be alive to-day with the colour that's on you,' for my father was black and blue all over the body."

"Glory be to the will of God," says my mother, getting up to shut the door because the hen has returned with two others to the meal sack and if given any more freedom they may soon fly on to the table and break the ware as I have often seen them do, "they say a person always goes black in the skin after a visit from the Good People."

I shivered when I thought of the fairy pinches.

" 'Tis no good sign either when they start talking to themselves in a fainting fever;" says Maura, "but leaving that as it is, however, Father James prayed over him till a sweat came over his reverence and shortly after that, with the will of God, my father recovered the use of his hand."

"Glory, honour and praise to the Holy Name," says my grandmother, making the Sign of the Cross, "isn't it great power the priests have in them after all is said and done!"

"It is, indeed," says Maura; "great power without a doubt in the world. But God help us, by the same token, they say they must suffer themselves for it after they cure a person like that."

"They say so," says my grandmother. "I suppose that is to remind them not to abuse their power of interfering with the will of God unless it is always done from pity or the love of God Almighty."

"I bet that step below the house was avoided for a long time after that, Maura," says my mother, rubbing her eyes, because now that the door is shut the chimney has less draught and the smoke begins to spread all over the kitchen so that we are all feeling miserable. The smoke seems like the cat, the cattle and the hens—it takes advantage of us when we are in a tight corner. It is always the same on cold days. If we happen to shut the door to keep out the sharp winds the smoke soon makes us open it again when we feel like rabbits being suffocated in a burrow.

"Nobody went near it by night for years after that," says Maura, sneezing, for the smoke is getting the better of her too.

"Go down, Brian, and open the door," says my mother, "or we'll stifle to death."

I go down at once and open it wide.

"Stand there a minute, my boy, and keep out the blasted hens," and my mother gets up and hands me an old shovel she has in the corner for removing the ashes.

"Is it steel?" I ask in all seriousness for fear another fairy woman might come along in broad daylight and bring in the hens by force.

The three women burst into a hearty fit of laughter and of course I feel annoyed and puzzled but I say nothing in case the fairy stories finish with my small self using the shovel on the living instead of on the dead.

"God be thanked for the fine fresh air," says Maura, wiping her eyes with the corner of her apron. "But to return to my story, why. When my brothers went down to the step the morning after the ghost appeared they looked about and could see nothing only a strange substance like jelly on the spot where the scytheboard fell."

"It is a bad thing to be out late, Maura," says my mother, "and I'm always telling that to Jim when he stays too long playing cards."

27

"Yerra, yes," says Maura, "but then, on the other hand, you see, a man must have some sort of amusement after his hard day's work."

"That reminds me now to hurry up with his dinner," says my mother, putting aside her knitting and building up the fire.

"Do you know that little bush below the road near the ruins of the famine houses east there, Maura?" asks my grandmother.

"I do, of course, woman," says Maura. "You mean that little wizened old whitethorn that grows beside the big grey stone, don't you?"

"That's the one," says my grandmother, "and between here and the Glade of the Saddled Horses you wouldn't find a more lonesome place."

"Why shouldn't it be lonesome, indeed?" says Maura. "Wasn't it a great number of souls that left these houses in the great famine, God bless the hearers."

"It was so, indeed," says my grandmother, drawing some sods of peat from under the settle and laying them beside the fire, "may God be good to them all. But I was thinking of something else. They say that in olden times a crock of gold was buried under the spot where that little bush is growing now. In the course of time a man dreamt about it and made preparations to go there by night and dig for it but, with the will of God, glory be to His Holy Name, before he could handle a spade, didn't he drop dead on the spot, God bless the hearers!"

"Look at that for you now!" says Maura, reaching with her stick for a few other sods to add to the ones my grandmother had already built about the fire which is now blazing brightly.

"Life is better than gold any day," says my mother, lifting a heavy pot of potatoes and hanging it on the crane over the fire. She hits some of the potatoes with her knuckles to bring them level with the water in which they are to boil, then places the cover tightly over them. She reaches for a flitch of bacon which hangs on the beam overhead and cutting some of it into slices she puts them to steep in a dish on the table, then hangs up what remains of the flitch.

" 'Tis good to have the meat," says Maura, turning her eyes to the loft where a good supply is hanging.

"I'm telling you 'tis no black eye at all," says my mother, sitting on the stool and resuming her knitting.

Now that the fire is blazing brightly there is little fear of smoke so I am told to shut the door again. I am right glad to be relieved of my job. I return to the hearth expecting to hear more fairy stories. But I am disappointed, for the conversation has turned to everyday things.

"What are eggs this week?" asks Maura.

"Ninepence a dozen," says my grandmother, "and there is a strong rumour that they're going down to sevenpence next week. These blasted shopkeepers are the devil's own rogues. We never know what they're up to with their twisting prices day by day."

"Wisha," says Maura, "God help the poor struggling farmer working like a slave from one end of the year to the other and then getting the lowest penny for everything he sells."

"Yes then," says my mother, "and paying the highest for everything he buys; living from the hand to the mouth and always at the mercy of the crooked gombeen men."

"Yerra, the devil carry them," says Maura, stamping her foot on the ground, "they have the whole country robbed with the height of trickery and blackguarding."

"Cut the top of the ear off me," says my grandmother, "you'll find it will all go bad from them in the end for they say the devil is good to his own in this world and bad to them in the next."

"What time is it?" asks Maura, standing up. "I must be off now."

My mother looks at the alarm clock which stands in a wooden box nailed to the wall over my grandmother's coop. "It is a quarter to twelve," she says. "Wisha, what hurry are you in, Maura? Why don't you wait and have a spud with us?"

"I won't indeed then, thank you, Annie. What brought me down at all was to borrow a pincheen of sugar till I get some at Gurthagreenane on Thursday when I take over the handfuleen of eggs and get whatever few pence I can for them. Have you any grain to spare?"

"I have, to be sure, and plenty for ever," says my mother, going to the dresser for a cup. "I had to borrow some last week myself from Nancy Taid for I had no one to send to the shop.

29

It would be a poor world indeed if we could not help each other now and again."

"It would then, surely," says Maura, smoothing back the hair under a little plaid shawl she was wearing about her head.

"I keep it above in the clevvy," says my mother, reaching for a big blue paper bag on the mantleshelf. "It stays nice and dry there."

"Don't put a heap on it," says Maura as my mother pours some into the cup. "I might spill it going up the curragheen."

"Very well, Maura," says my mother, handing her the cup which is full to the brim.

"God increase your store, my good woman," says Maura, "and a hundred thousand thanks to you. I'll bring back the cup when I'm returning the sugar."

"All right, Maura," says my mother.

"Good day to you all now," says Maura, going out with the cup in one hand and the stick in the other.

"Good day and good luck to you, Maura," we all say with one voice, "and may the road rise with you on the way home."

My mother took the slices of bacon from the dish and placed them in a pot-oven with a piece of lard. Pulling out a few red coals from the fire she placed the oven on them with a metal cover on top. Soon we heard a sizzling sound and knew from the pleasant smell that we were in for a nice dinner.

The water in the pot of potatoes had been boiling for some time and my mother lifted the cover with the tongs to see if they were boiled. Placing the cover against the wall she dipped the tongs into the pot, took out one of the potatoes and squeezed it in the end of her sack-apron with her fist. "They're done," she said, putting back the potato and laying down the tongs. Reaching for an old sack from under the settle and holding it around the hooks to prevent getting burned she lifted the pot from the crane and laid it on the ground. Then she stuck the hooks into the handles of the pot-oven and hung it over the fire. She laid the sack across the top of the pot of potatoes, covering it all except a few inches at one side and, lifting it up, she turned it over a bucket which contained some Indian meal and drained off the water. After this she laid the pot of potatoes on the cinders from which she had taken the oven and left them there to dry. She stooped under the table for the gruelstick and stirred the meal in the bucket to make porridge for the pigs, already grunting at the door.

All being ready she pulled down the hanging table and placed a clean meal-sack on it. She went out and stood on the step below the house to call my father from his work in the fields. When he came in he sat in his usual place beside the hanging table. My mother got the old sack again, lifted the pot of potatoes and said "Bear a hand." We all held up the verges of the sack on the table to prevent the potatoes falling on the ground when she turned them out of the pot in their skins which were cracked and bursting from the heat. A few of them stuck to the bottom of the pot but they soon came loose when she struck the verge of it sharply on the table. I liked potatoes with burned skins. She laid the pot on the floor in front of my grandmother's coop and taking the oven of bacon from the fire she divided out a share to each person. It smelled lovely with the onions which were cooked with it and it was not long before we were all lapping it up. We peeled the potatoes with our finger-nails, my father alone using a little black worn old knife he had found in the ditch some years before. We had a most enjoyable meal. The potatoes were lovely and dry. We called them Yellow Champions and they always grew well in Coomlaegill. We finished with cups of milk and while we puffed and belched we would not call the king our uncle. What more could anyone want?

IV

The Wise Women

M

Y sisters and I were fond of asking questions. My
father did not like it, because his knowledge was
limited. He seemed to think that a desire for information was a sort of disease and that it was a sure
sign of insanity. In our valley an illegitimate person, old or
young, was always called "a by-child." Confusing this with
"boy" I wondered why some, even girls, were alluded to that
way and others were not. Finally I said to my father: "What is
a by-child?" He put me off and did not answer. My grandmother was more willing to help. When I heard her saying that
Larry Mulvanny had to marry our cousin Kitty O'Falvey I
asked her why. "Because she was going to have a child," she
said. That satisfied me although I had no idea that Larry had
anything to do with it beforehand. I took it for granted that the
child came to Kitty of its own accord and that Larry married
her because men had to marry just as they had to smoke, drink
or dig potatoes. My mother laughed when she saw my father
embarrassed with my questions, but I kept on asking just the
same.

When it came to questions about the other world my grandmother was like a complete information bureau. She seemed
to know everything about spirits. By all accounts they had been
about a lot in her time. She spoke of them as if they were every-
day people. They were not so plentiful these late years, she
said, because of a powerful prayer the Pope had ordered to be
said after Mass, for he had had a vision of millions of bad
spirits who "wander through the world for the ruin of souls."
This prayer, she said, sent them back into hell.

We gathered around her after dark and then she began:

"In olden times the people of this parish had no doctor and
when anyone got sick they sent for the wise woman instead."

"What is a wise woman, Nanny?" asked Eileen from her
perch beside the cricket-crack.

"A living person who is in the fairies at the same time."

"God save us, Nanny," said Eileen, her mouth wide open and a look of fear in her big grey eyes, "what do you mean by being 'in the fairies'?"

"I mean, my bright child, that she could see and hear as well as talk to them. She was a friend of theirs and went about with them from place to place by night."

"Oah, woah," said Bridget, shivering beside me and squeezing her arms across her chest, "I wouldn't like to meet her at all."

I shared the thought as well as the shiver.

"You'd be better away from her track too," said my grandmother, "for you'd never know when one of her companions would put his eye on you and want you to join them."

"If that was the way with her then why did people send for her?" asked Bridget.

"Well, my girl, why do they send for the doctor now?" said my grandmother. "People will do anything to save their friends and relations from sickness and death, and sure, indeed, putting this and that together, maybe sometimes a wise woman is better than a foolish doctor."

"What did she do when they sent for her?" asked Eileen, pushing suddenly back from the fire which had started to crackle and send out sparks in her direction.

"You're going to get money, my little girl," said my grandmother, seeming to ignore her question. "It is always a sign of that when sparks fly towards you."

"I'd rather it without the sparks," said Eileen.

"So would the rest of us, indeed," said my grandmother, "only I'm afraid while we're in this world we must always keep knocking sparks out of something like the smith at his anvil before we can get the money. But to get back to the wise woman—you asked me what did she do when people sent for her. Well, a gilla gal, sometimes she came to see the sick person and sometimes she did not. The Lord between us and harm, the like of her was a fright to the world for telling things."

"What kind of things, Nanny?" I asked, thinking that maybe she told people where the fairies hid their gold.

"Oh, my bright boy," she answered, "she told them what they wanted to know very much."

"What was that?" I persisted, for I was too young to know the weight of sorrow that pain and sickness brought on families.

"They wanted to know, poor creatures," said my grandmother with a mournful sigh, "whether the sick person was going to live or die. You don't know the troubles of the world yet, my boy. God keep the knowledge from you for many a long day. You'll have time enough to cry when learning comes your way. When there is danger of death in a house relatives will hang on to any trifle giving hope for the patient's recovery. That was why they sent for this kind of woman. She could tell them secrets from the other world for she got her knowledge from the fairies."

"Did you ever know any of these women?" I asked, for I was full of curiosity about them.

"I did, indeed, my boy. It isn't long ago at all since one of them lived near the road to the bogs of Slievemore. Her name was Mary O'Mara. She used to get the falling sickness, God save the mark, and it was while the fits were on her she could tell the future like a sainted prophet in the Holy Land. She saw so many things that it seems they went to her head in the end, for too much knowledge is a bad thing, surely, and she set fire to her little house while her husband was lying in bed. With the will of God he woke up in time and the poor little maneen escaped, but Mary herself was burned to death, God rest her soul."

"Oh, wasn't it terrible," said Bridget.

"Dreadful out entirely," said Eileen.

"I knew an aunt of hers as well," continued my grandmother as we gathered closer to her knees in case Mary O'Mara came down the chimney in flames to rush at us like the sparks had flown at Eileen, "and she was far better than Mary for telling the future. She lived in a little house also near the lonesome bogs not far from where I was born myself."

That made the story more interesting for we all felt that my grandmother must surely have inside knowledge of the other world on account of having lived so near to these distinguished old women, drank tea with them, perhaps, walked to the market with them and what not!

"I remember Biddy O'Mara as well as any person I ever knew," said my grandmother. "She was the fine nochass woman,

God rest her, and a fine housekeeper too, not like more of them that wouldn't put out the cat at night or the hens in the morning," with a side glance at my mother, for they were still rather cool after a recent squabble. "My father and mother were away at the fair of Kenmare when my grandfather got sick, God be merciful to all their souls; I hope they're in heaven to-night. They took me with them for I was the youngest and left my two brothers at home to see after things about the house. They were about fourteen or fifteen at the time. They hadn't much sense any more than ye have now but my grandfather was there to advise them if anything went wrong with the cattle outside. God help us, he was that feeble himself that he could only sit in the corner and give directions. Well and good, why, sometime in the evening he was struck with an awful headache, God bless the hearers. They put him to bed below in the room. He warned them to tie in the cows and to see that they didn't horn each other in the crow. He told them also to have spring water brought in for the morning because nobody knew who might be calling during the night. He meant the Good People, of course."

"Mother of God protect us," said Eileen in great wonder, "do they come in at night like that?"

"Faith then, they say they do, my girl, and 'tis always better to leave the hearth nice and tidy for them."

I had often seen my grandmother sweep the fireplace immediately before going to bed, moreover during wild and stormy weather when, she said, the dead might be coming in for shelter. If they found the place untidy, she added, they might talk about it among the neighbouring pookies, because the dead have endless time for gossip.

"They say the fall of night and the rise of dawn are favourite times for pookies to show themselves," continued my grandmother. "This night the dark was just after coming when one of the boys heard the tramp of a horse's hooves coming up to the house and stopping at the door. He jumped up and got excited but his brother heard nothing. They got afraid, God help us, the creatures, and why shouldn't they, indeed? Often and often they were after hearing it said that the fairies won't be seen or heard by one out of every three that are present when they come. They ran into the room, my love for them,

35

and jumped behind my grandfather in the bed. By the same token, it is the very bed I sleep in at present."

I shuddered when I thought of all the nights I had got into it in the past as these boys had done. I even feared going into the bed in the loft but there was no way out of the trouble except to sit by the fire all night and have a holy host of dead ancestors around me in their long brown habits and white lonesome faces freshly risen from the graveyard at Gurthagreenane.

"I'd die with fright," said Eileen, scratching her head with a vigour that showed the presence of little creatures that were anything but dead.

"You would not then," said my grandmother, "nor the devil a die. Neither did my brothers for it was not long before my grandfather comforted them and told them to go up and open the door to see who was there. He was after hearing the clatter of the hooves as well. They did as they were told but could see neither man, woman nor horse. They heard nothing either, the creatures; nothing in the wide earthly world only the distant moaning of the river, the piercing cry of the curlew and the kheening whistle of the lonesome winds."

"What did they do then?" I asked with a shiver.

"They came in quickly, you may be sure, and shut the door with a bang."

"I wouldn't have the courage to go to the door myself at all," said I, moving still closer to my grandmother.

"Ah, you're an old coward," she said, pouting. "You're not like my people at all. The O'Sullivans were as bold as brass."

"H'm," said my mother under her teeth, as much as to say: "That goes without telling."

My grandmother was one of the O'Sullivans of Bohereen-fhadda before she married my grandfather.

"I'd be afraid too, Nanny," said Bridget.

That made me feel more comfortable.

"And I would as well," said Eileen. "But what happened then?"

"As soon as my father and mother came home," said my grandmother, "they had a talk with my grandfather and could see that he was very sick. They got a fright too, you may be sure, for sudden deaths follow the family, God bless the hearers, so they went for Biddy O'Mara the following day. I remember

36

well to see her coming in. You may say that she was the fine respectable woman in her black hood-cloak and snow-white cap. She had a hazel stick in her hand. I thought she had it to defend herself from the cattle on her way across the bogs. There was more to it than that, may truth be with me, without a doubt in the world."

"She could beat the bad pookies with it, I suppose," said I, remembering what I had heard Maura Nee Lhaera say about it.

"Something like that my boy," said my grandmother. " 'Twas a powerful weapon like the Rod of Moses. Anyhow, to make a long story short, she went down to see my grandfather. He welcomed her, of course, for they were old friends."

I felt proud when I heard this, thinking it great that so close an ancestor should be friendly with a woman so well in with the pookies. I felt that if ever I met them in the dark, and God forbid that I should, I could say to them while the bones were shivering in my skin: "Come here a minute. Wait a whileen." And I wishing them a thousand miles away at the same time. "Didn't you know my grandmother's grandfather? He was a friend of Biddy O'Mara's." That was, of course, provided my voice didn't die within me from fright and that I did not melt away into a piece of jelly like what was found where Maura Nee Lhaera's father stabbed the fairy woman long ago.

"Was she a relation of yours?" I asked.

"No, indeed, my boy. She was just an old neighbour."

"What did she say about your grandfather?" asked Eileen.

"I'll tell you then, my girl. When she came out of the room she put the hasp on the door as easy as ever she could and moved towards the fire in the kitchen. I was watching every move she made. She pushed out her jaw and pressed the lips against her teeth. She put the hazel stick in the corner under the horse's collar that was drying on the hob at the time. She had a very serious look on her face like a woman going into a churchyard. 'What do you think of him, Biddy?' said my father. She squeezed her lips tighter than ever and waved her hands to and fro. 'I'm afraid,' she said, folding her arms and nodding her head to one side. 'I'm afraid of him. He's a very sick man and you want to keep an eye on him.' My father looked at her earnestly for her gaumees told him she was hiding something. 'Tell me now, Biddy,' says he, 'in the words of an honest

37

woman, what is your opinion about him?' She shook her head and began to hesitate. 'Well,' says she at last, 'since you want to know, my good man, I may as well tell you and stop my beating about the bush. The man is old, God help him, and the days are made. I don't like to discourage you, but, between you and me and the wall, I'm afraid poor Darby O'Sullivan is no more.' My father got a shock when he heard this, and why shouldn't he, indeed? 'What makes you think that about him, Biddy, a lhae?' says he to her. 'Well then,' says she, 'I'll tell you now and be done with it. His brother Curney came for him on a white horse last night. He must go. There is no getting away from it. They want him to play in a big hurling match on the other side and he must be with them.'"

"Where was Curney living at the time?" I asked, for I had often heard about the great white horse the O'Sullivans had long ago.

"He wasn't living anywhere, my boy. He was dead and buried with eleven years!"

"Oh, Lord," muttered Eileen, shuddering and scratching her head again. "Dead eleven years, is it? And was the horse dead too?"

"Don't mind the horse a whileen, my girl," said my mother, suddenly interrupting. "I know by the way you're scratching your head all night that you're ate alive with boodies." Standing up, she reached to the clevvy for the small combeen. "Come here a whileen till I rub this through your hair."

"Ah, can't you leave me alone till I hear the story?" pleaded Eileen for, like all of us, she hated having the comb drawn through her tangled hair to get under the creepers.

"You can hear it over here just as well," said my mother, taking her across by force.

"Was the horse dead though, Nanny?" asked Bridget, keeping track of the story.

"He was indeed, a caileen, stone dead at that, and for a long time before Curney too."

"What did they want hurling for when they were dead?" asked Eileen, during a short rest from the comb.

"I don't know, my girl," said my grandmother, "any more than why they want to do it while they're alive. But if a living person happens to pass by the hurling field and one set of players ask him to play with them he must go in and play like the hammers of hell. If his side loses the game he must die at once for the other team will sweep him with them in spite of the others."

I shivered when I heard this. I wouldn't have the ghost of a chance in a game with the living not to mind the dead with jaw-bones flapping on their habit-collars and open coffins parked along the ditches, unless I could fall back on the friendship of Biddy O'Mara and use a little blarney for the sake of getting off.

I asked my grandmother what happened after Biddy had told them that my sick ancestor was no more; and the words "no more" were puzzling me for I could not understand the mystery of death which made a living person be as nothing again.

"She advised them to send for the priest at once," said my grandmother, "and have the poor man prepared for the long journey before him. They did as she told them and, sure enough, with the will of God, he was dead and buried that day week, the Lord have mercy on his soul this night and for ever."

"I suppose the pookies told her what was to happen," said Eileen, during another break while my mother stooped over the fire to throw in the careless creepers the little comb had caught napping.

"Of course they did, a gilla," said my grandmother. "That man was carried as sure ever that horse came into the yard."

"What do you mean by 'carried'?" I asked, being anxious to learn all about these things in a world where I might one time have to meet with them.

"Come over here, you lousy rascal," said my mother, "till I draw the combeen through your hair in case the boodies carry you and your sisters down to the river and drown you like unwanted kittens in the blackness of the deep."

I had to take my turn, much against my will, for the rack went slowly through the mass of twisted curls on my head and the pulling made a soreness that the boodies never knew.

" 'Carried' means being suddenly swept out of this life by the Good People," said my grandmother.

"Carried by the Boodyman is every bit as bad," said my mother, referring to an ugly old pookee usually mentioned to

39

frighten children and sometimes used as a nickname for a dull and rough-looking man.

"Could the people carried never come back?" asked Bridget, preparing her hair for combing when her turn came.

"Sometimes they could," said my grandmother, "but it only happened rarely. When the fairies took a person in good health, as they often did, God save us, they left a useless image behind in place of the person taken. If the living person was wise enough not to eat the food the fairies put before him he could return to this life if his cursed image could be frightened out of its wits in one way or another. The fairies dread fire, water, steel and hazel. If Brian Boru himself with Fuan MacCool and all their followers swept a living person they must return him in fawning fear of these four powerful things that make the hearts go crossways on the spirits of the dead. That is why an attack on the image with a red-hot poker, shovel or frying-pan will drive the fairy frantic. He will run back to the liss with a fright for ever in his heart. The living person will return in his place if the trick is done before the fairy pressure and the pains of hunger forces him to eat."

"What would happen if he had just started to eat at the very time the image was running out of the house?" I asked as the last comb-load of boodies was hurled into the fire. I certainly did not want them replaced by others from either this world or the next.

"The fairy image would die on the spot from fright. Then the police would make enquiries and maybe charge the relatives with murder. So you see the getting back was always a tricky business."

"Did the person using the hot poker say anything to the image by way of no harm at the time?" I asked, anxious about the fine points of everything and a great nuisance for asking questions.

"They never said one word, my boy, until the poker was red-hot. If they did, a Muirra, the changeling would walk out and give word to the fairies. Then they'd kick up holy murder in the liss, start threatening the living person and make things so awkward for him that in the heel of the hunt he'd have to take the food and then he was gone for ever. So the relatives at home kept his image in the dark, then suddenly stabbed at him with the poker, saying at the same time: 'Come back, Brian O'Shannissey,' or whatever his name might be, 'come back, Brian O'Shannissey, in the Name of God!' "

These words frightened me for my own name was Brian O'Shannissey and it was often I had heard my people call after me when I was in danger: "Come back here, Brian, in the Name of God!"

"Did you ever know of anyone like that to come back?" I asked, resuming my place at my grandmother's knee while Bridget took hers for the final combing at my mother's.

"I did, indeed, my boy. There was a woman above here some time ago, Norry O'Loughlin was her name, and a fine sober swaulkuc girl she was in her day too, before the meddling fairies took her. But if they did why, she wasn't gone long when a wise woman advised her relatives to take her image to the top of the ivy-covered rock that's drooping over a deep black pool in the river at Corrigafeephawn and throw her in suddenly, saying the usual prayer to God, glory be to His Holy Name, and to have a good swimmer ready to save her from drowning, for fear of the law as well as the fairies. They followed her advice and after the terrible shock of a sudden fall into the dark water, out came my Norry as fresh as a daisy with the will of God and the help of the man that rescued her. From that day to this she never looked back. She married the same man afterwards; Con the Piper they call him. They're living beyond in Bantry now and I'm told they have a fine family of boys and girls, God bless them and spare them from the troubles of the world."

Our house was a perfect setting for the telling of these stories. Outside lay the black expanse of gloom with here and there a nodding bunch of furze bushes that looked for all the world like a crowd of fairy women and they whispering in the wind. Inside was a cosy kitchen with a blazing peat fire on the open hearth and a small sickly paraffin lamp lighting without any glass protection for the flame. This was called "the small lampeen" and was taken about the house whenever it was needed. It was made from tin shaped like a bell with a brassy covering. It made a lot of smelly smoke. For special occasions, however, as when my father wanted to point spars for the thatch, we had a big paraffin lamp with a glass chimney but

41

even that showed only a dull light because the damp air had a bad effect on it. "Mind the lamp, you devil, you!" was the usual warning if any of us went near it and were likely to forget where we were. Whenever these lamps ran out of oil the house was left in semi-darkness. It was then we thought of the pookies in the loft overhead and in the room below. We dreaded moving about in case one of them might put his cold and clammy hand upon us and then go laughing back into his grave!

V

The Black Art

WHEN my father had done the spring ploughing he smoothed off the ridges with an adze-like implement called a "grafawn" made by a local blacksmith. While he was at this work my mother and grandmother were busy in the kitchen. They drew a sack of potatoes near the fire, for the weather was cold, got two sharp knives with the tops broken off to square the ends and tied rags about the handles to protect their hands from the rough verges. Sitting opposite to each other on low stools they began to cut the potatoes into pieces called "skhilawns" for planting. Each piece contained a sprout which was called an "eye." Making a triangular cut around each eye they sunk their knives deeply and removed them with some of the potatoes attached. They put the sprouts into a bucket containing a little lime. What remained of the potatoes were called "creelickawns." These were put into a separate vessel to be boiled for the pigs and cows. They took as many as six or seven skhilawns from some big potatoes.

As this is a slow and tedious job a neighbour would often come to help. So down the rock came Maura Nee Lhaera with her usual smile. She was made welcome of course for we knew her business. She drank a cup of tea but wouldn't take any food.

"Damn the skin of it, Maura," said my mother, putting a plate of bread and butter beside her on the settle, "won't you have one little mouthful before you start cutting?"

"Upon my soul then, I won't, Annie," said she, taking off her check apron and replacing it with a clean meal-sack my mother had given her.

"Will I boil an egg for you, Maura?" asked my grandmother.

"Yerra, Lord bless you, no, girl," said she, reaching into the pocket of her long blue flannel skirt for the special "skaineen skhilawn" or little sprout knife she always brought with her for the job. "That it may kill me stone dead if I tasted a sign, and that's hard enough on me now after I cursing. God be praised for all His goodness, sure I'm only after leaving the table this blessed minute above at home and, the dear knows, it isn't sparing the food I am at all, may the Lord increase your store, indeed, my good woman."

"Wisha, aren't you very strange?" asked my mother.

"I'm not indeed," said Maura, putting on her glasses. "And by the same token now it isn't eating or drinking that brought me at all but to help you on with the skhilawns."

"May God reward you for it, my good woman," said my grandmother, already seated on her stool for the job.

Maura peered through her glasses, took them off and wiped them with the corner of the little brown shawl she was wearing about her head and shoulders. Then raising them up in front of the window, she looked through them again, gave them another wipe, put them on and sat down beside my grandmother. A big zinc bucket of potatoes stood between them and they began to cut out the sprouts as fast as my eyes could follow. My mother sat with them now and again to help but not for long because she had to attend to the baby, prepare the dinner and so on.

"You're lucky to have your field ploughed before the weather breaks," said Maura.

"The dear knows then that's what we were saying the other day," said my mother, "and we may thank the good neighbours for helping us."

"Ah, well," said Maura, "we may as well help each other, for it isn't long we'll be together, God help us. Our cousin, Barney, west here, is ploughing to-day too."

"What field is he ploughing, eroo?" asked my grandmother.

"An unlucky field then, the Lord save us—the liss."

"Unlucky is the word for it without a doubt," said my mother. "I often heard the old people say they never plough that same field but a cow dies on them before the year is out. That's as sure as ever they turn a sod on it."

"Oh then, that's no word of a lie," said my grandmother, speaking in a friendly way, for she was on good terms with my mother at the time. "I'm after seeing it happen more than once myself since I came to Coomlaegill."

"Nobody should ever interfere with any of these lisses,"

44

said Maura, "and that one in particular. I often heard tell of a little old man that was minding his cow near it in olden times. He used to fall asleep at the job and when he'd wake up, with the will of God, the cow was nowhere to be seen. The following day she'd be back but the devil a drop of milk she'd have. Well and good, why, one morning he swore by the stars of heaven that he wouldn't go to sleep if the cat went to pound but that he'd keep a tight watch for the thief that was stealing the milk from his cow. Everything went on well for the first few hours but around twelve o'clock the cow began to get very uneasy. He thought the flies were playing on her, perhaps. At the same time he felt himself getting very drowsy and he had the devil's own work trying to keep his eyes open. Eroo, with that he saw her moving towards the hole going down into the liss but if she did, why, he made one drive after her and caught her by the tail to keep her back. Faith and sure, there was no stopping her. She pulled him down after her as easy as ever you like and when they were below didn't he find himself in a lovely room where everything was bright and shining like a new pin. A door opened and out of another room came a beautiful young woman with a pail in her hand. She smiled to him as sweet as you like and he began to feel himself getting weak. He wanted to ask her why she stole the milk but he could not get himself to do so because she had stolen his heart as well. That's the way with the men always, God help them. He lost his speech completely as soon as she put the 'Come hither' on him. She pointed to a lovely book with a golden cover lying on the table between them. 'Take that,' she said, 'in payment for the milk. It will tell you how to get in and out of here whenever you want to.' The old man looked at the book and shook his head. 'I can't read,' he said feebly, for his voice was coming back. 'It is just as well for you, my dear man,' said the lady, 'if you're content without it. But maybe your childer will want to read it.' The old man looked at it again but was afraid to touch it. ' 'Tis a costly book by the looks of it,' says he, 'and surely you can't give it to me for nothing.' The lady smiled for she knew the old man had a weather-eye for bargains. 'I'm not doing that at all,' said she, 'for I want your cow in return.' The boot was on the other foot then. Like all farmers the old man thought the world of his little coween. 'I can't let you have her,' says he. 'A golden book is useless to a man that cannot read but a man that never saw a page of writing can milk a little cow.' The lady saw that she was losing but she did not give up. 'There's a power of wisdom in your proverb,' says she, 'but I suppose you know that you're in my power at present and that you're a trespasser in a world to which your kind does not belong. You must pay a price to get out. As I see you don't want to leave me the cow, I'll ask you to make another bargain before I can let you return!' The little old man was like a rat in a trap, God help us. He was losing courage again but in a different way. 'What is it?' he asked, shaking like an ivy leaf. 'I'll tell you then,' says she, 'I'll tell you. From now on whenever the owners of this farm dare to plough and plant a crop over my liss they must lose a cow to pay me for the loss of this one.' The old man was astonished but he kept his senses where a younger man might lose them. 'One cow at present is worth ten in the future,' says he, 'and I'll be pleased if you'll let me keep this one. I know her but I don't know them. Far-away cows aren't always the best milkers.' The lady looked at him in surprise. 'I can see, my good man,' she said, 'that even though you cannot read you have a very sound argument. So you can have your cow after I have milked her for the last time.' The old man was delighted. She sat down on a little stool and began milking the cow into the pail. While she was doing so she started singing a fairy song in such a lovely way that he forgot where he was and fell asleep. When he woke up he found himself lying beside the liss and the cow grazing in front of him. She never again lost her milk in the same way but, ever since, whenever that field is ploughed, a cow is sure to die on the farm before the year is out."

"Praises be to the will of God," said my mother, going up to the loft for another bucket of potatoes.

"I wonder was he wise in refusing to take that book?" asked my grandmother.

"Yerra, God help your head, girl," said Maura, "there isn't a farmer living that wouldn't rather a lame cow or a hungry pig more nor all the books from here to The Lake of Learning in Killarney."

"That's true for you, indeed, then, I suppose," said my grandmother. "A cow with good produce in her milk is worth looking after, I'm telling you. God guide and guard us, they say that some people have the power to charm the produce from other people's dairies. Maybe that book was telling how to do it, for a woman that could coax the cow into a liss could coax the cream into a churn."

"I don't know, a lhae, Joan," said Maura. "There must be something in it all the same. There was a family above here some years ago that had the name of being able to carry the butter from their neighbours. They borrowed or stole the coulter of the plough from these people and kept it reddening in the fire while their own butter was being made. You may be sure that it was then the butter would come in plenty while the owners of the same coulter could make none at all if they churned on till the crack of doom. The coulter helped to culti-vate the land producing crops for the cattle and the good luck of the farm went with it. Another member of the same family, God between us and harm, went to the graveyard at night, opened a coffin with the help of her friends, took out the dead hand of a spinster, brought it home and kept it hidden in a cupboard until she was preparing to churn. Then she stirred the cream with it and a strange power from the other world increased the butter beyond measure."

"God protect us," said my mother, returning from the loft with the potatoes. "Isn't it terrible what some people will do for gain after all!"

"Yerra, God help your head, girl, that's no notice," said Maura, who had great knowledge of these things. "They had hundreds of other tricks as well for getting at property without taking it in the open. Some of them kept a young goat with their cows to bring good luck and they say this charm would not work unless the kid was stolen! Even the young men tried to charm the girls in the same way. The best known one of them was Mike the Colleens. They say he used to keep a little box of devilment called 'coaxiorum' in his pocket and while he had it with him there was no girl safe in the place! The Lord save us, some of them had power over life and death as well. One of the O'Mara Moors above here fell sick of a time. There was no hope in the wide world for him until his aunt called to see if she could do anything for him by charms or something. They say she had some trucking with the Good

47

People or maybe the devil himself, the Cross of Christ between us and the dirty beast. She knew a lot about these little herbs that grow in the fields and ditches, however in the world she came by the knowledge, nobody knows. She said one of them would cure him if it could be pulled with safety but any creature pulling it would die on the spot. The disease would then be removed from the sick man to another. She thought of a plan, with the devil to help her, I suppose, for he always stands at our elbows in cases like that. So, getting the tip from Old Nick, she tied one end of a string to the herb and the other to the leg of a gander. God be merciful to us all, when the poor bird flapped his wings with the usual 'gee hig' and ran away from her he pulled the herb with him and dropped dead on the spot! The woman went towards him at once, took away the little herb, boiled it slowly with a few other little biteens of devilment and gave the juice to the sick man to drink. With the will of God, when he had it drank, and a bitter lot it was by all accounts, he felt a new man and as lively as a bee. He was fully recovered but, God bless the hearers, at the same time, didn't a fine hearty young man of a neighbour giving them a day's work in the paurkeen beside the house get struck down with paralysis, God save the mark, and die in a few days' time."

"That's what they got for trucking with the devil," said my mother, while I felt the hair standing on my head with fright in case some other old woman might be tying a string to a gander's leg at that very moment and that it might be my turn to fall as soon as she had the soup ready for the patient who was to recover at my expense.

"Do you remember old Pad Bwee, Annie?" asked Maura.

"I don't then, Maura. Do you mean the great piper?"

"I do, indeed. He was before your time, I suppose. He was a great man entirely for the charms and he played lovely on the fife as well as on the bagpipes. I own to goodness, Annie, I'm telling you no word of a lie, his music would coax an angel from his harping in the halls of paradise itself. He was a gifted man surely. He was always sent for whenever a horse got the farcy or any other bad disease like that. He asked the woman of the house for a little butter and put it into a bottle. He muttered something that sounded like a Latin prayer as he shook the bottle and kept a close look on the butter. He was a seventh son, you see, born on Good Friday and christened on Easter Sunday. People like that do have great power always. Well and good, why, with the will of God, when the butter turned into blood, my Pad would up and tell them that the horse was cured. That was a solid fact, as sure as you're there, for when the owner went to see the animal in the stable the farcy was withered away and the horse was fit to jump the stars with life and strength and taspy!"

"Glory be to the will of God," said my mother in great wonder as she stirred the fire under the pot of potatoes she had previously hung on to boil.

"Maw sha then, he was a great poet too," said Maura, emptying the bucket of skhilawns into a kishawn which had been placed below the end of the table for the purpose.

"They say that poets never have a day's luck," said my grandmother.

"Maybe some of them don't deserve it either," said Maura, sitting down and cleaning her glasses again, "for they make bad malicious verses when a rust comes on their temper. By the same token, Pad had the power of sending the crooked luck to others too if he took the notion. People were in mortal dread of him on that account, and small blame to them, for they say he could raise a crop of mangy blisters on anyone he didn't like by twisting words of poetry in the corners of his mouth."

"May God protect us all," said my grandmother, striking her breast.

"Did he ever do it to anyone you knew, Maura?" I ventured, suddenly remembering that I had a little patch of something like ringworm behind my left ear and beginning to think that maybe some new poet was beginning to practise the black art on me in the quiet.

"He did then, upon my soul, my little brightness," said Maura, "and did far worse too, im breersa fain. He was at the pattern in Gougane of a time and while he was out walking with a young woman didn't a fellow from this parish make himself busy enough to steal an ivory fife that was given to Pad by a landlord as a present for curing his racehorse. My Pad got drunk during the night like many another man of his time and forgot all about the fife. He was so bad that he had to be

helped home across the mountains before day. He was getting
sober by the time he reached the top of Eskwee, a bleak and
dreary hillside above the waters of the lake of Saint Finbar,
for a long journey on the bare and lonesome boglands would
sober up a giddy goat not to mind a drunken piper. It was
then he missed the fife and kicked up holy murder about it.
When he found out for certain that it was stolen he was like
a stinging wasp on a war of vengeance. With that he sat down
and began composing like a hatching hen goes pinching when
her nesting is upset. He twisted himself about on the bawn-
sheen like an animal in pain, cursing the thief in a song that
brought a sweat of anger to his brow, wishing that the lightning
from the vaults of heaven might come down and kill him in
his bed before either priest or parson could prepare him for the
life beyond the grave. God Almighty guide and guard us, it
was a terrible sight: the grey dawn stealing over the great
brown mountains with their gloomy shadows, and an angry
piper making rhymes like that! And, the Lord between us and
harm, it wasn't long too till the curse fell on the poor fellow
that stole the fife, Dhoanal Na Cheira above here, God rest
him, for he was killed by a flash of lightning in the bed while
his wife lying beside him escaped without as much as a single
spark touching her body."

Maura went on from story to story as bucket after bucket of
potatoes was cut into shape for planting until it was time for
dinner. My mother then went out to call my father and when
he came in he gave a hearty welcome to the visitor. Standing
on his heels he tapped the toes of his heavy hob-nailed boots
together in a lively fashion to shake the soil from them. Then
he took an old birch broom from behind the back door and
swept the soil out into the yard. I noticed his patched and worn
trousers, especially at the heels where the strong leather pulling-
up thongs of his boots had worn channels in the home-spun
flannel which was of the herring-bone pattern, and his grey
wrapper that, by the way, had been sewn together for him by
Maura some weeks before.

"Have you any news for us?" he asked her as he sat on his
usual place beside the hanging table which my mother had
just taken down.

"Now then that you asked me," said Maura, taking off her

glasses and putting them on the window-sill for safety, "maybe I have and, by the same token, I forgot to tell it to your mother and Annie. Your cousin Daniel O'Neary's daughter is getting married next Saturday to a man in Ballyvourney."

"For goodness' sake, eroo, is that so?" said my mother. "Do you mean the good-looking girl?" for it seems the O'Nearys were a mixed lot, some of them being anything but handsome. I was supposed to resemble the plain batch and I did not like it at all.

"She is then, indeed," said Maura, "and she's no shame to them wherever she goes."

"You took the word out of my mouth," said my grandmother. "Why shouldn't she be good-looking, eroo, and to be anything to her father, a fine decent respectable old man?"

He was her first cousin and she thought the world of him and his family.

"Oh, wisha, God help us then," said my father, who did not share his mother's views about old Daniel's beauty, "is it that old fellow? I own to the devil this day, he reminds me of nothing in the wide world but the blasted old pookee that goes around dirting on the blackberries!"

"Haw, haw, haw!" went Maura into a hearty laugh in which even my grandmother joined. "The Pookee Na Smeeroiga! Haw, haw, haw! What a funny comparison! The devil wouldn't beat you, Jamesy!"

The Pookee Na Smeeroiga was a fairy my sisters and I had a special grudge against, for the old people told us that he went around dirting on the blackberries every Michaelmas Night and that we should never eat them after that time of the year. We thought him a very nasty old creature and wished he could find a convenience somewhere else besides doing harm to the fruit.

After Maura had taken her dinner with us she continued cutting the seed potatoes until late in the evening when she went home.

That night I asked my grandmother if Biddy O'Mara, the wise woman, was related to the O'Mara Moors.

"She was, my treasure," said my grandmother. "Old Dansel Ogue, God be good to him, the present O'Mara Moors grandfather, was Biddy's uncle, so you see how near related they were."

Then I remembered Paddy O'Mara Moor who went along the road muttering to himself. People thought he was conversing with the fairies. My grandmother told me that when he was a boy he slept out of a night—a very eerie thing to do, she said—and the pookies lifted him holus-polus off the ground, flew with him across the valley in a wheelbarrow and left him sitting on the verge of a dangerous rock on the opposite side where his people found him after a long night's searching and shouting his name. He got a bad fit of sickness out of it, and small wonder, indeed, she said. He spent nine years in bed and was never again the same. My sisters and I enjoyed listening to him as he went along, wondering what he was talking to the fairies about. Bridget and I were never afraid of him for he was quiet and friendly whenever we met him on the road. But Eileen dreaded him and always ran whenever she saw him coming along, the brown hair sticking out under his big grey woollen cap, and making a great clatter on the roughly-gravelled road with his heavy hob-nailed boots.

"A lot of the O'Maras seem to be in the fairies," said I to my grandmother. "Does it run in families?"

"Indeed then, it does, my boy, the same as any other disease, like sweaty feet, red eyes, madness or poetry."

"Oh, my goodness!" said I in surprise. "I didn't think poetry was a disease!"

"It is then, and a very bad disease at that, moreover when the poet takes a fancy to a girl while the schomull is on him. My word for you, there is no peace for him then, God help us, for if he marries her, the cure is often worse than the disease!"

I opened my mouth wide, completely bewildered. Small blame to me, indeed, for I was surrounded on all sides by the bordering dangers of two worlds while being warned about them through the bordering idioms of two languages. Between the fairies with their changelings, the wise women with their hazel sticks, the butter-charmers with their skeleton fingers, the herb-women with their screeching ganders, the pipers with their farcy-curing bottles, and the poets with their evil-wishing poetry, it was little sleep I got that night, I'm telling you.

VI

A Little Learning

BRIDGET and Eileen started going to school a long time before me. I was nearly seven before I went with them. My health was poor. That was why I was kept at home so long. As a result of not being robust I was fonder of staying in the house listening to the women talk about spirits and witches than of being out in the fields listening to my father talk about cattle and crops. I had never seen any books except the one in my mother's trunk and the little school-books my sisters learned their lessons from. I have a hazy idea about seeing the remains of a more advanced book with dog-eared corners and the picture of a man wearing a wig on one of its pages. It must have belonged to one of my aunts or uncles. It had disappeared completely by the time I began to understand what a book meant at all.

I asked my grandmother about school.

"You'll be learning to read and write there," she said. "You must begin with the small words such as 'Tee oh, tu' and 'Gee oh, go.'"

That sounded sensible.

But my mother came along later on and told me I should first learn the Alphabet. That big foreign word sounded strange to me. I did not like it. It seemed so meaningless that I decided on learning the "Tee oh, tu" and "Gee oh, go" first and letting the Alphabet look after itself.

Books were scarce in our valley because farming people did not care for them. They preferred cattle and pigs instead for they knew that reading books was less profitable than rearing animals in so far as making money went. But as each farmer knew that most of his family should go to America later on he saw to it that they got as much learning as would enable them to write to him when they were gone, even if someone else had to read their letters for him should he not be able to do so himself. If an old man here and there went beyond the limit and

53

started reading more than his neighbours he was looked upon as being upset in the head and became an object of pity with some and ridicule with others.

I was anxious to know what the school at Gurthagreenane was like and I expected it to be a thatched house like our own. I was surprised, when, on asking Eileen about it, she said it was like a hay-rick! If it is like that, said I to myself, how can the scholars get into it? I concluded that they just sat around it and learned their lessons there. A cow-house would be better than that, I thought, moreover in rainy weather, but as I was too far away to solve the mystery for myself I was under the impression that it must be something in the disguise of a hay-rick at any rate.

Now, however, the day came when I started to wear my first pair of trousers and, after I had practised putting them on and taking them off a good many times each day, in the long run I felt myself master of the puzzle. They were made for me by a girl in Gurthagreenane without ever seeing me. Her name was Alice. She also made the habits for the dead.

When my sisters saw that I could get in and out of a trousers they concluded that it might be safe to take me to school. My parents thought otherwise for they saw that I was still much below normal for my age so they decided on keeping me under their protection for some time longer. But that did not please me at all. Now that Alice had a little jacket made for me with brass buttons on it I began to get a little impatient to see the scholars' hay-rick and also the wonderful village of Gurthagreenane where all the houses stood together like a bunch of cattle, as I was told, and not like Coomlaegill where two or three fields lay between one house and another. I remember that each of the brass buttons had an anchor across its face. My mother was born near the sea and perhaps that was why she got me these buttons. On top of all that she crowned me with a sailor's hat!

I was now fully dressed. There was nothing for the sailor but to start on his first voyage into the great unknown world. My sister Eileen, a year younger than me in age, a year older in wisdom, must have seen that I was still a bit wild so she decided to take me on a practice journey of an evening; the trousers and jacket acting in place of the martingal, I suppose! She walked me along the great rough winding mountain road, pointing out the wonders on the way: The Fairies' Rock; The Pool of the Frogs; O'Grady's Kiln; O'Mahoney's Gullet; O'Sullivan's Turn; and finally, after what seemed a very long walk, the most wonderful sight of all—the great village of Gurthagreenane, seventeen houses all together in one bunch on the top of a little hill surrounded by lovely green fields! Lord save us, I got a fright! I had never seen so many chimneys clustered in one place. The red bricks made them look like the mouths of some cranky old smokers I knew in Coomlaegill. A little to the west of them I saw a big new white building with what seemed to be a tin gallon can with a conical top where the chimney should be! Wonders will never cease, said I to myself, looking at the whole scene, for the spot we stood on was opposite the village and right over the river which ran westward through the lovely wooded valley below. I asked Eileen what kind of a house it was that had the tin can for a chimney. "That's not a tin can," she said, looking at me in surprise. "That's the new chapel you're looking at and the thing like a tin can is where they keep the bell!"

When Bridget heard that I could really walk so far with my new suit on, and that I did not throw stones at any windows on the way, she and Eileen decided that it might be safe to chance taking me off to school unknown to our parents. I was willing enough myself, of course, being the fool I was, having no idea of what I was walking myself into. The following morning, therefore, I went off without my parents' leave or blessing and lived to repent it soon enough, I'm telling you. In spite of my sailor's suit the voyage was on dry land; very dry at that, for it was a beautiful sunny morning in early September and the road was hot and dusty. I could hear the little streams running through the heather on the hillside and the lowing of cattle in the fields. We drank heartily from a little well on the roadside. I felt very tired because my sisters travelled faster than usual so as to be in time for school. However I carried on bravely enough until we reached Gurthagreenane where the houses looked very tall and stately with their painted fronts and big shop windows. At last we came to the middle of the village and there was the school! Imagine my surprise when I found that it was not like a friendly hay-rick at all but a great dreary-looking building with mighty big windows, so different from the ones at home. There was nobody sitting around it as I had expected; who would care to sit around a prison? It looked like one, surrounded with great thick stone walls six feet high. It didn't even smell like a hay-rick! We went in through the great red iron gate, opened sparingly from the street. When I was inside, like a rat in a trap, my sisters gave me a further shock by telling me to go into the boys' school which was on the ground floor while they went upstairs into the girls' school. I went shyly in and stood beside the door, my cap in my hand, my head hanging and my spirit at the bottom of my heels from bitter disappointment.

It was not long before the Head Master saw me and asked me where I had come from.

"Coomlaegill, Sir," said I, looking fearfully into his eyes, having been warned at home not to forget the "Sir."

"Oh, I see, my boy," said he. "The Valley of Bright Love!" for that is the English for Coomlaegill. "The Valley of Bright Love in the mountains above! What is your name?"

"Brian O'Shannissey, Sir."

"A son to James O'Shannissey?"

"Yes, Sir."

"Very well, my boy. I'll put you in the Infants' Class."

He took me into a smaller room where his brother was in charge of about twenty little boys who were sitting before him on terraced seats.

"Another addition to the family," he said to the brother, and then he hurried back to look after the bigger boys who were making a lot of noise.

I looked in front of me at all the strange faces, the bright light from the big windows gleaming on everything in the room.

"What is your name, my boy?" asked the Assistant Master, catching me by the forelock as you would a donkey, and you may be sure that I felt like one too!

"Brian O'Shannissey, Sir, from Coomlaegill."

"Oh, I see. We have another boy of the same name in the school already," said he, giving a pull to the forelock, "and we must make some distinction."

I thought he was going to invent a nickname for me but he

did not. Instead, he let go the forelock to my great relief and started to walk up and down in front of us while I was carefully eyeing the cane he carried in his folded hands behind his back.

"I've got it," he said at last, coming towards me with a smile.

"Got what?" I asked in a loud voice like I would at home, forgetting the "Sir," and all the boys laughed with the Master.

"What I have been trying to think about," said he. "Your mother's name is MacNeill, isn't it? Annie MacNeill?"

"Yes, Sir."

"Very well then. We'll call you Brian MacNeill O'Shannissey; then when you hear me calling the rolls later on you won't get mixed up with your namesake."

I was wondering what "calling the rolls" meant for I had often heard my sisters talk about it. I had a hazy idea that it had something to do with calling out the names of the scholars but I could not figure what they were called for. I was puzzling in my mind if it could be done in the same way as my parents called the cows, and whether the Master used any special word for it such as "Sup, sup, sup," as they did to the cows.

He put me sitting at the end of the lowest seat with five or six other little boys, all smaller than myself, for some of them lived near the school and their mothers sent them in to be out of their way. I felt very lonely in the new surroundings, but after a while the Master came over and gave me an encouraging pat on the shoulder for he could see that I looked despondent.

"Brian MacNeill O'Shannissey!" he said, rolling the words about in his mouth with emphasis on every syllable. "Brian MacNeill O'Shannissey! What a splendid name! As Irish as the Blarney Stone!"

Then he gave me a halfpenny which was a big sum for a small boy who had no money.

"When were you born?" he asked, catching me by the fore-lock again.

"I don't know, Sir."

"Very well, Brian. Ask someone at home to write the date on a piece of paper and bring it to me to-morrow," and he gave an extra pull to the forelock again so that I should not forget.

"To-morrow, your hat!" says I in my own mind, for I had no intention of coming to-morrow or any other day either.

I was wondering too if my people would know when I was

57

born for birthdays were never celebrated in our house. Nobody in the valley ever bothered about them as far as I knew. However, I had an idea that my mother often said that I was born around the same time as the November fair was held at Kenmare. Jamesy O'Loughlin of Coomlaegill was born on the same night but he had started going to school a year before me because he was a fine healthy boy. Each year our birthdays came and went without as much as an extra wag of a dog's tail to mark the events. On that account people lost track of when they were born and then, when they wanted to go to America or get married or take any other steps in the pathways of danger, they had the devil's own bother running here and there to this person and that who had a sick cow or a sore elbow at the very time the searcher was born. By reason of the particular trouble they might remember the date and give it to him or her to take to the office of the steamship company or the parish priest as the case might be. A search would also be made perhaps in the "Process Box" in the house being called to. These boxes usually contained bills, summonses and rent notices as well as processes. It might be on the very day of the birth that the summons or process-server was seen going towards a particular house by the baby's father on his way for the midwife and then, twenty years after, when the need arose, he would connect the two events and call to the house for information, hoping, no doubt, that someone might perchance have made a note of the birth on the back of the process, having more time to do it than he had in his hurry and excitement.

Sometimes the farmer, it seemed to me, was not sure about the number of children he had himself, leaving out the bastards altogether. So his careful wife would cut a notch on the verge of the cradle every time a new child came to sleep in it. They counted sheep on a stick by the same method. They were, on the other hand, very careful to make a note on paper of the time they expected a cow to calve or a sow to farrow. They were very careful too not to count their chickens even after they were hatched! It was an unlucky thing to do, they said.

I felt very lonely in school and thought it awfully queer having to sit for such a long time without even talking. What does it all mean? I asked in my own mind.

"You must bring money for books and pencils, too," said the

Master, disturbing my thoughts. "A ha'penny for one of these," he added, pointing to a little red book with black printed writing on the cover which the boy beside me had in his hand after reading his lesson from it. "A ha'penny for a lead pencil and a ha'penny for a slate pencil. Now, don't forget to bring three ha'pence with you to-morrow."

Heavens Almighty, said I in my own mind, it must cost a fortune to make a scholar!

The standard coin among schoolboys was a ha'penny. Everything in the place seemed to cost a ha'penny. The shops were crowded with ha'penny toys. The baker sold "a ha'penny bun" to one boy and "a ha'penny duck" to another. Even the Master who now stood before me had a ha'penny cane in his hand, in spite of the fervent prayers of countless schoolboys past and present that the price might some day go beyond his means!

While the Infants were on the bottom seats the boys in First Class were on the higher ones. They were nearly all strangers to me except the boys from Coomlaegill who sat among them. As the Master called on them they stood up one after another to read the short and simple stories from their little books. They were anything but simple to me at the time, of course, because I could not read a single word.

Having little to do on my first day I kept my eyes on each boy as he stood up. I remember one of them in particular. He was a policeman's son wearing a striped white-and-blue jersey over his lanky waist. "Long, long ago," he read, "when London was a small town there lived in it a boy called Dick Whittington," and he went on with the story of the cat, stammering here and there until the Master called out "Next!" and another boy continued the story. That was the first time I heard of London and I said in my own mind that if it was much bigger than Gurthagreenane it must be a fine town now!

When playtime came we all went out to the school-yard and I stood beside the gate looking for my sisters. As I waited there, who should come in but Joan Mulloy from Coomlaegill. I was very glad to see her. She handed me a hot ha'penny bun with a shiny-brown sugary top which my thoughtful grandmother had asked her to take in to me after she had found out that I had gone off to school without taking any lunch with me. I was so full of excitement all that morning that I had forgotten food altogether. But you may say that my appetite returned when I smelled the nice hot bun and it was not long until I had finished it, I'm telling you.

While I waited in loneliness, one of the Head Master's sons, a boy about ten years old, came along and gave me a friendly pat under the chin. He was a gentle boy and I have liked him ever since. The other boys in the school were a mixed lot. One of them came and asked for my name. I told him. Another came and did the same. I told him also. Five or six others followed and I told them all, never suspecting that it was a little schoolboy conspiracy to have fun at my expense.

At last the girls were let out to play in a separate part of the yard and I was greatly comforted when my sisters came running over to ask how I was getting on. I was so delighted at seeing them that I said nothing to Eileen about the missing hay-rick! They warned me to wait for them outside the gate when school was over so that we could be going home together.

Back in the school it was the same thing over again. Lessons and silence for half an hour each time, at the end of which the Head Master would clap his hands briskly as a signal for one set of boys to stand up, leave their seats to make room for others, then march in an orderly line either into the small room or out of it to some other part of the school where they marked time until the Master told them to stop. Some would stand in a ring around the rostrum where he sat on a high stool with books and papers in front of him while others would sit at the desks behind them. All this orderly marching was a big surprise to me for I had never seen the like of it before. We did everything by fits and starts in Coomlaegill and there was nobody to order us all to do the same thing at the same time.

The small apartment with the terraced seats was called "The Class Room." It had only been built a few years and its light-brown ceiling had a look of newness about it which I thought would last for ever. In fact I thought everything in the whole place would last for ever because the time seemed so long while I was there. I looked up at the ceiling in its great height and compared its brightness with the sooty blackness of our loft at home. The huge windows, opened and shut by cord, ratchet-

wheel and bar at the top, also attracted me and the big brown
ventilators high up in the walls were a mystery to me for I had
never seen anything like them before. Sitting on the end of the
little low form I thought of many things but my thoughts were
interrupted when the Master said suddenly: "Give out slates!"
One of the bigger boys stepped from his perch above me, went
outside the door and came back with a pack of smooth rect-
angular slates. As he walked along from seat to seat each boy
took a slate and rubbed the front of it with his palm. I took
none because I did not know what they were for but I watched
the others carefully.

When all the boys were ready the master called out a set of
figures and they wrote them down. One boy, however, sat still
and did nothing. The Master asked him what was wrong. "I
have no pencil, Sir," he said in a mournful whine. "What
happened to the one I gave you yesterday?" asked the Master
sharply. "I lost it, Sir," said the boy. "Hold up the hand here
to me," said the Master, and for the first time I saw the cane
being used. "That will teach you to mind your pencil," added
the man with the rod as the boy started to cry, rub his hands
together and squeeze them between his knees. I knew then
what I was in for myself if I forgot the three ha'pence. The
Master reached to the table for a slate pencil lying there and
handed it to the boy who seemed to have forgotten his trouble
already. His name was Denis O'Keefe and I thought he looked
a bit reckless compared with the others.

The Master called out a second set of figures and told the
boys to add them to the first. There was dead silence and I
could hear the boys muttering under their lips. This muttering
seemed strange to me for I had been used to hear the boys of
Coomlaegill say everything out loud.

The Master gave me a slate and pencil to amuse myself
with. I was delighted though I did not know how to write a
single figure. However I thought the Master a rather decent
sort of man and then forgetting where I was I said out loud:
"What's your name, Sir?" My voice seemed to ring through
the school and my question was answered by a roar of merry
laughter from the boys in which the Master could not help
joining. They were all so used to hearing the Master ask the

61

boy for his name that their fancy was greatly tickled on hearing the boy ask the Master for his! "You must not ask questions like that in school, Brian," said the Master. "You must learn to keep silent like the other boys." Then I realised that school on the inside was no more like home than school on the outside was like a hay-rick!

The weight of restraint which this queer silence put on me was so great that I became more determined than ever not to go to school any more. I was sick and tired of the long standing, sitting, marching and thinking. Seven happy years had passed almost unknown to me at home where everyone was full of love and kindness and where I always had freedom of speech; but now, alas, the other side of life was beginning to show itself.

There was great joy in my heart when the classes were over at last and I went outside the gate to wait for my sisters who soon came along and formed a bodyguard to take me home safely. "Never again!" said I with a frown when they asked if I would go to school on the following day.

When I arrived home I got the welcome of the world with the same gentle sort of talk that you never hear in school. I was greatly disappointed, however, when my parents insisted on my going back to school the following day. I knew then what a fool I had been to go there of my own accord on the first day! I had nobody to blame but myself, I thought, and that was poor consolation, the dear knows, for there was no way out of the trouble but to submit.

That evening I went out and had a good look at the hay-rick in the haggard. It seemed so homely and friendly compared with the school that I could have sat down beside it and cried like a Jew at the Wailing Wall in Jerusalem. Three or four little calves bellowed at the other side of the fence and I envied them their freedom which I had shared up to then. There would be no silence, no slates, no figures for them to-morrow or the day after either. The mystery of life began to be more puzzling than ever before. What was the meaning of school at all, at all? I kept on musing in this way for so long that any sensible person would be justified in asking if a two-legged calf had been added to the list during the day!

In spite of it all the sun was going down in the golden west as if nothing had happened and when it had disappeared completely behind the deep blue rim of the lovely mountain peaks I went sorrowfully back to the house.

After supper I went to bed and slept soundly all night, thank God, in spite of the fact that fairyland for me seemed shaken to its very foundations.

VII

The Beginning of Trouble

STRANGE to say, when I went into school on the second morning I felt more at home than I had done on the previous day. I was greatly pleased with the new book and pencils I had bought at a little shop kept by the Assistant Master's wife with the post office opposite the school gate. This woman, my grandmother had told me, was a cousin of ours. That comforted me. I felt that while I had Biddy O'Mara to plead with the pookies I should have the postmistress to do the same with the Masters!

Now that I had a slate like the other boys the Head Master sent his son to guide my hand with his while I wrote the letters and figures which he showed me how to form with my pencil. His own writing was excellent and I learned quickly under his guidance because he did not get angry when I made mistakes.

I learned the forbidding Alphabet slowly but it was a key I needed if I wanted to read and write. Having got over that stumbling-block in the course of time I was soon taught the "tee oh, tu" and "gee oh, go" my grandmother was after telling me about. Then came "an in, an" and "oh ex, ox." I thought myself a profound scholar when I came to the big lesson beginning with "Jack has got a cart" which every boy in the parish seemed to know by heart. This made trouble for the Master. Boys would stand up and read in a sing-song fashion which showed him that they were not actually reading but repeating from memory. Two little sentences always gave the game away. "To hoist is to pull up" was one of them. It had a full stop at the end. The sentence following was: "Joe toils the whole day long." Unfortunately for all concerned Joe happened to be at the end of a line so that when the scholar came to repeat this part of the lesson he ignored the full stop because he did not fully understand what it meant. When he carried on, depending on luck, and rushing like a ploughing horse to the end of a furrow, what he actually said was: "To hoist is to pull up Joe!" Heaven only knows how many times the boys were pulled up for pulling up Joe before the Master could make them understand that he belonged to another sentence!

While learning my lessons I watched what the other boys were doing. A group would gather around a blackboard resting on an easel at the end of the big schoolroom. The Master would take a piece of chalk and draw a figure on it like the gable-end of O'Sullivan's hay-shed which I had seen on my way to school. A boy would point to each side of the figure in turn with a shiny stick, saying: "This and this are equal to this and this" as he pointed to particular lines, "therefore this and this are equal to this and this" as he pointed to others. Another boy would take his place at the board, acting and talking in the same queer way until I had heard so much about "this and this" being equal to "this and this" that I hardly knew where I was with my brains going round and round like a dog hunting his tail! That figure would be wiped out with a cloth and the Master would make two dots about four inches apart on the board. Pointing to each dot in turn he would say to another boy: "With this as centre and this as radius, describe a circle." The boy would take the chalk and draw a ring on the board with one of the dots in the middle and the other in the rim, using the same kind of talk as the others. Paddy O'Mara Moor's conversation with the fairies seemed very simple now compared with all this rigmarole. At least he knew what he was talking about but I'm afraid some of the boys did not any more than I did myself.

Out at play again I was asked for my name several times and when Maurice O'Grady of Coomlaegill saw what was going on he came to me and whispered that I was a fool to have answered. He was a year older than me and knew the ropes. I felt puzzled as I did not know what to do instead of answering. "When they ask for your name the next time," said Maurice, who was a cute little boy, "say 'Butter and craime' like the others do. Then they won't ask you any more." I tried this when the next boy came along and he was so disappointed when I did not answer in the way he expected that he got angry and would have hit me if some of the bigger boys had not stopped him. When the others found that I gave them the same answer they gave up asking and turned their attention to another new boy.

A popular school rhyme contained the answers to most of the questions likely to be put to newcomers. It ran like this:

QUESTION	ANSWER
What's your name?	Butter and craime.
What's your fancy?	Sugar a' candy.
Where were you born?	In the cow's horn.
How've ye the praties?	Big and small.
How do ye eat them?	Skins and all.

"How've ye the praties?" is a great question among the farmers when they run short of a subject for conversation.

There was a singing lesson each day carried out with the help of a modulator, charts and tuning fork. The Master tried me on the modulator and found that I had no voice for singing so he put me aside with a group of boys called "Non Singers" who usually went out of the class-room while the others sang, it being out of place to keep the crows among the nightingales. I was very disappointed when I found I could not sing as I wanted very much to do so because I was very fond of music.

The Master struck the fork on the table, then held the end of it to the wood for some time. "Tong wu hoo, oo, o, o, o." The vibration it made in the air was like a long musical sound coming from the ceiling. While it lasted the Master would sing out a list of letters from a high to a low note: "C . . . B, A . . . G, F, E . . . D, Doh," order the boys to "take the note," whatever that meant, and begin to sing with them, usually "The Harp that once through Tara's Halls" or "The Songs our Fathers Loved." Sometimes he would begin: "Taa; taa; taffa teffy. Taa; taa; taffa teffy" which was very puzzling to me. It reminded me of the "Muck; muck; mucka mucka" sows made when feeding their young.

It was bad enough for me to find things awkward in school and to dislike it from the start but it was on the way home that I suffered most when my sisters were not with me. The boys knew I was a coward on account of my poor health. They picked at me whenever they got a chance. They never did it singly but always in batches. The more I showed resentment the more they threw stones at me or pushed me about. I suffered most from those younger than myself. They had the powerful backing of the bigger and stronger ones who prompted

66

them for the pleasure of seeing me suffer. Finding that I was over-sensitive they called me names and said filthy things about me which made my days and nights a misery. Maurice O'Grady, Jamesy O'Loughlin and a few others were decent boys who sympathised with me and were never cruel but they ran most of the way home and I could not keep up with them. We had three classes of boys on the Coomlaegill road: one running; one lingering; and one taking the middle course. I usually travelled with the last-mentioned but sometimes I would be delayed and fall into the hands of my enemies, the lingerers.

However, in spite of all my troubles, I soon found myself in First Class and then in Second. I was now under the Head Master, Curney O'Shea. He was a very serious-looking man with a sharp red face, bushy eyebrows and a greying moustache slightly waxed at the sides. He was very quick-tempered and ready to lash out with the cane at any time, having it always held behind his back as he walked up and down the school talking to his brother while we did our lessons. When he sat on the rostrum examining copy-books he had it always before him in case he came across bad writing or spelling as he turned over the pages. He had two sets of spectacles; one with smoky lenses for walking about; the other for reading. These had clear lenses and when he wore them I could see the red wrinkled flesh about his eyes. He looked much crosser then, perhaps on account of the extra strain on his eyes. It was always a sure sign of a coming storm when he put them on. Some unfortunate boy would be called before him and get two strokes of the cane on the palms of his hands. His cane was of a shining orange colour, costing twice as much as the one used by his brother and lasting twice as long in spite of the fact that it was sometimes stolen by some daring boy and pushed through a crack in the floor or hidden somewhere else when he turned his back or went outside. When he missed it he would fume and rage, buy another if he could not find it and use the new one with a double vengeance.

When these temporary outbursts were over, however, he became quiet again like any ordinary man minding his cattle and sheep in the peaceful countryside. He walked about repeating verses to himself or staring at the ceiling in profound thought. He had a very poetic mind and a great knowledge of Greek and

Latin. He was always anxious that the boys should learn the connection between these languages and the English they spoke in school.

I can hear his black polished boots creak loudly as he walks along the floor in his dark striped suit, stiff white collar and red tie. He wears a beautiful yellowish-pink tea-rose in his button-hole. When I see it I think of his lovely house in front of which there is a great profusion of these roses which I can see on my way to and from the school. They are over-shadowed by two stately horse-chestnut trees under which he and his family sit on summer evenings. He muses as he walks along:

"Sweet Auburn, loveliest village of the plain,
Where health and plenty cheered the labouring swain."

As I struggle with my lessons I feel I am another labouring swain though there is nothing to cheer me but the slowly-moving hands of the little yellow-faced clock standing on a corner-bracket to the right of the rostrum and pointing its long hand to the end of each half hour. The creaking boots draw nearer. I know he is beside me now and, oh horror, the creaking stops! He must be looking at my copy-book, I think, as I shudder and lift my eyes to the level of his golden watch-chain. I can see the sovereign hanging from it as an ornament. I expect him to say in an angry voice: "Hold up the hand here to me," as he has often done before. But I am mistaken. "The thoughts of youth are long, long thoughts," he muses again as he walks away to my great relief. But after a few minutes the creaking sound draws nearer again. He stands beside me and repeats the same words, followed by a friendly pat on the shoulder which makes me jump nervously. "Aren't they, Brian?" he asks with a twinkle in his eye which I can see under the smoked lens. I am too stunned to answer. I feel the hot blood run into my face. I do not know what my own thoughts are, long or short, because of the fright I get when I see his bristling moustache so near me and his teeth showing in the act of smiling. But he does not wait for an answer. Away he goes, repeating:

"A boy's will is the wind's will,
And the thoughts of youth are long, long thoughts."

Sometimes his wife would come into the school with his

lunch when the servant-girl was away. If he happened to be in one of his pet rages at the time, she would rush up to him, hold his hand and save the boy concerned from a caning. We all loved her for this and were always glad to see her. She had been a teacher herself before she married and was a woman of a very high intellect. She kept an interesting collection of the world's greatest books and was always ready to lend them to people in search of knowledge or the way to better things.

There was one subject which I was expected to learn and failed to do so. That was Algebra. If Euclid was Greek to me, Algebra was gibberish. I could make neither head nor tail of it and, to be entirely frank, I failed to see where anything could be gained either in this world or the next by letting X be equal to it!

At parsing too, I must admit, that as a failure I was a great success. I hated it like rank poison and could never see the use of tracing the relationship of one word to another, moreover when it had to be done in a language more puzzling than that of the sentence being parsed. I saw no point in it apart from that of driving young minds to the verge of madness and thought it a great waste of time to be bothering with it at all.

Only for the help of a friend called Clarence O'Reilly, smaller and younger than me, I would be completely lost and have to suffer countless "paudies" as we called strokes of the cane. The Head Master was growing old and getting very deaf. It being a bad wind that blows nobody good, I took advantage of his failing by listening to the whispered promptings of my friend who knew the subjects and repeating like a parrot what he said in a loud voice as if it had come from myself.

Clarence was by leaps and bounds the cleverest boy in our class, if not in the whole school, but for some unknown reason the Head Master did not like him. His sister was a teacher and, no doubt, that was a great advantage to him when learning his lessons at home. Unfortunately the Master seemed to enjoy punishing him. Whenever he slapped him he added to the boy's trouble by jeering. "Come up here to me now, my little tom-tit," he would say, calling him out before him, and down would come the cane with an unmerciful slap. "Take that now, my little tom-tit," he would add with a vicious glare in his eyes. Still not satisfied, when he saw Clarence crying and squeezing his palms between his knees he would call our attention to him: "Let ye look at him now, my little tom-tit!" and point the cane at him in derision. I pitied poor Clarence, and this cowardly treatment made me wild against the Master who, though quick-tempered, was otherwise by no means a bully. I could never understand his attitude towards this brilliant boy. Like so many other things in the school it must remain a mystery for ever.

I had another friend in our class also, a very gentle cultured boy who could speak Gaelic. The Master, who could also speak it, was fond of conversing with him. His name was Finnawn MacNulty. He lived in a cottage near Harping's Castle, owned by a local landlord. Finnawn told me he had often visited the place. "There is a statue of the devil inside the door," he said. This did not surprise me because sometime previously, on seeing the tall grey castle tower with a big dark window showing over the tree-tops and looking in the distance like the head of a man with his mouth opened I wondered what it was and asked my grandmother. She said it was the devil! Harping was a Protestant and I believed that all members of that persuasion for some reason or another had a high regard for Old Nick!

Because I was of a shy retiring nature most of the boys thought I would never have the pluck to hit back and that they could push me about whenever they pleased for the amusement of onlookers as well as themselves. Denis O'Keefe, already mentioned, was a very poor scholar and extremely careless. He was always picking quarrels with the boys. We all disliked him on that account. He had a curious habit of sucking the middle finger of his right hand, briskly rubbing his upper lip with his forefinger at the same time. So when a boy wanted to pay him back for his insults he said nothing but stared at Denis in front of the other boys, put his fingers to his mouth and used them as he did. That was like showing a red rag to a bull. When the other boys burst out laughing, Denis rushed at his enemy, lashed out on all sides and usually kept at it until the Master came and stopped him. He was younger than me but hardier. He was very friendly sometimes but he was liable to change like the weather. One day I was sitting quietly in the class-room when all of a sudden he attacked me without rhyme or reason,

70

first with his tongue, than with his fists. I flared up at once. The Master was absent, of course. My temper rose to its highest pitch and I lost control of myself completely. I took hold of him, shook him violently, knocked him down and beat him heartily with the bag of books I had with me. An Irish temper is a jewel sometimes. When he cried for mercy I let him go. From that day on he never interfered with me. All the others were delighted and offered me their congratulations for having beaten the bully of the school. But with all his faults he had one fine redeeming quality. He was the very soul of generosity. While hitting you with one hand he might have a bag of sweets ready for you in the other. He divided good things with everybody. He was ready to give the shirt off his back to anyone in need. I have never known another child of his age so good-hearted and that gives him a never-ending glory in my eyes.

The last lesson each day was Catechism. The Protestant boys attending our school left before that began. I did not like learning the answers by heart because both questions and answers were made up of very big words. There was a list of meanings at the top of each chapter but even the meanings were puzzling in themselves. At least I found them far beyond my poor knowledge. I had a fairly sound idea of the first five Commandments of God but when it came to the sixth I was in a haze, though I had a vague idea that adultery had an important place in matters of sex. I don't think any other boy in the school knew what it was but as little, though I daresay they all knew how it was done! They had slang names for everything connected with sex which they talked freely among themselves but I could find none of these words among the meanings in the Catechism. That left me so much in the dark that if I had actually committed adultery I would comfort myself in thinking that it was something else and that I did not know the slightest thing about the great sin mentioned in the Sixth Commandment!

When I read "Thou shalt not covet thy neighbour's wife" I was still more puzzled. What did a man want coveting his neighbour's wife for if he had one of his own already? I asked myself. And if he had none of his own, why covet another man's wife when he could find another man's daughter? The Catechism said nothing about a neighbour's daughter, so that I felt there was nothing wrong in myself wanting to get friendly with Rachel O'Hara, a very beautiful girl who lived near the school. Her father was a policeman but that made no difference. He couldn't be always keeping guard over her. But alas, when I met her on the road and nobody else there but the two of ourselves she ignored my presence and turned her dreamy eyes towards a pig that was rolling in the mud at the other side. She knows I am only a country caubogue, says I in my own mind as she passed me by in stony silence, her footsteps giving glory to the ground she walked upon, and I dragged my weakening limbs along the other way, gasping in an effort to stop myself from swallowing the Adam's Apple in my throat!

VIII

What Happened out of School

MY sisters and I went to school in our bare feet the whole year round except when there was frost or snow on the ground. We felt much lighter without boots, tripping along like the birds, our hearts as light as theirs. But now and again I would strike my toes against the rough broken stones freshly laid on the road to keep it in repair. I would leave a trail of blood after me while a big piece of flesh hung from the wounded toe which would fester later on and be the cause of misery to me for weeks. My big toes usually suffered most in this respect. Just when the wound would be on the point of healing, some boy would accidentally step on it with his hob-nailed boots as we lined up to get into school in an orderly way after playtime. That would add another few weeks of misery to my troubles. Sometimes this would happen immediately before a heavy frost so that I could wear no boots while it lasted. Then, no sooner was my toe completely healed than another boy would step on my heel and drag off a strip of flesh which in turn took a long time to heal.

These troubles were bad enough, the dear knows, but they were accidental, and I bore nobody any malice on their account. But my sneaky persecutors on the way home cashed in on my misery for their own amusement. They threw stones and gravel at my sore feet for the crude pleasure of watching me jump about with pain when they hit the wounds. This type of persecution was carried on to such a pitch that in the end I could stand it no longer. One of the chief trouble-makers, tired of his usual game of prompting the younger boys, now came out in the open and threw stones at me himself. I had suffered years of misery from this particular boy and one of his brothers who had now happily finished going to school. My temper flared when I saw the well-known sneaky smile on his face as I winced from pain caused by a stone he threw. My rage knew no bounds for it had been pent up for a long time. I also felt

73

much stronger now than when I first went to school. I went to the fence, seized a big stone I found near it and flung it with all my might, hitting him right in the middle of the back. He fell to the ground, poor fellow, shouting to the others: "Catch him! Catch him!" But they did not catch me for I ran like a hare with the hounds after it. From that day forth the bully was as quiet as a lamb towards me and so were the others. I felt very sorry for what I had done to him but I could see no other way out of the trouble.

During the holidays and week-ends my sisters and I were fond of wandering on the hills, especially in the summer when we went to pick whorts and blackberries. We often visited the great heathery valley near Kill in Coomlaegill. It was hidden from the roadway and looked majestic in its loneliness and beauty. It lay between two great purple mountains and a clear stream flowed along its base which was usually covered with a light-blue fairy-like haze in the heat of summer. Through this an occasional dragon-fly of a slightly deeper blue would float gracefully towards us, followed presently by another as if the fairies were sending them out to greet us. Countless butter-flies of various colours also fluttered about as well as millions of flies, big and small, whose wings, together with the mass-movement of wingless insects among the grass and heather made a continuous gentle buzzing sound which we noticed more than ever when we stooped to pick the berries. Above all this could be heard the distant gurgling of the stream with the occasional bleating of goats and the lonesome "baas" of sheep on the mountains overhead. Altogether it was a wonderful scene which I can never forget. I could see the lovely fresh green fields forming a picture gallery at Keownnafauil in one end of the valley with the farm houses in their sheltered nooks among them. Away on the other side lay a vast expanse of brownish-purple heather on the mountains with great white fleecy clouds moving slowly over them here and there.

The best whorts grew among the ruins of old houses which had been deserted after the great famine. Before that sorrowful event a little village stood here surrounded with tiny fields among the rocks. The outlines of these fields are still to be seen but most of them are now too coarse and wild for cultivation. It was a heavenly spot for a village of any kind, but alas, hunger has no regard for beauty. My father told me about an old man who once lived there. He had a little garden and when his potatoes put up their stalks the soil was so scarce that he could not find enough to cover the space between them as is usually done to keep down the weeds so he had to do the job with little flagstones instead. Curney O'Shea's ancestors lived near this village also before removing to Gurthagreenane. All is desolate now where once the voices of many people rang through the air. We thought of this as we plucked the berries from the little bushes between the stones and the lovely smell of the fruit reached our nostrils from the tin vessels we carried with us to hold them. The fairy haze was blue, the dragon-flies were blue, the sky above was blue, but our fingers and mouths were of a deeper blue than any from picking and eating the rich juicy berries.

When we grew tired of picking we stood up and looked around us, feeling lonely that our pleasant fruity picnic was coming to an end. As we moved away from the bushes we looked back and sighed, repeating a little verse we had made up ourselves, addressed to the friendly bushes and stones which we feared might not be there if we returned on the following year:

"Good-bye, good-bye to all of you, wherever you may be;
At home among the ruined walls or scattered on the lea."

Then we went home and handed the vessels of fruit to our mother who made a lovely pie with them for us. "Man alive, you'd eat your fingers after it," as my grandmother used to say.

Later in the year we went searching for wild plums and crab-apples. As none of these grew on our farm we went to steal them from our neighbours. Getting up at the first streak of dawn, unknown to our parents, we crossed the valley while the people slept. Then we crept fearfully on to the fences on which the plum and apple-trees usually grew, our eyes turning about in all directions lest the owner might swoop on us after having stayed out all night beside the ditch to watch for us! A pity for our heads, indeed! He had something else to trouble him at the time, but how could we know? Having filled our satchels we returned home, well pleased, and hid the fruit in the hay-rick to be eaten later on.

My sisters were very fond of going to school. By now they

75

were accompanied by my third and youngest sister, Abbey, who was a very delicate child. Until she was seven years old she was very healthy but one Sunday evening she became unconscious from sunstroke. I remember hearing my mother crying bitterly for she thought she would not recover. The doctor was sent for and after he had treated her she regained her senses with the will of God, though she never fully recovered her health. While she was sick the kind old neighbours came to see her. They offered advice to my mother about her. I remember Nancy Taid in particular. She was always kind to us when we called to her house and we liked the fine soft bread she gave us. She looked at Abbey lying in the bed, spoke to her in a friendly comforting way, an art in which all the local women excelled, then came up into the kitchen and whispered to my mother: "Yerra, 'twas some little flower she pulled. I saw her picking them west in the Beggarman's Field the day she got struck, God save the mark."

The field belonged to Denis O'Grady, Nancy's husband. It lay below a little pool called O'Grady's Well which was fed by a clear sparkling stream coming from the side of the hill. As I drew the water from it in a tin can after I had heard what Nancy said I looked fearfully over my shoulder at the great profusion of flowers below; marigolds, violets, buttercups, bluebells, mayflowers and big white cup-shaped plants called "Mock-an-dhaw-how." From now on I was going to be very careful about pulling any of them. Not me, indeed. I was going to leave that job to O'Grady's gander and I didn't give two hoots if it killed him either, for he was an impudent nosey devil that would let no child pass without stretching out his long neck, hissing like a snake and running after anyone foolish enough to be afraid of him.

But what am I after saying? Sure, upon my soul, even ganders had their good qualities, apart from losing their lives to save others in an act of witchery or greasing the palates of hungry talkers at match-making parties. According to the women of Coomlaegill the very breath they blew had virtue in it because it had all the essence of the little herbs and flowers they picked up to eat. So when babies suffered from thrush the gander's breath blown down their throats was said to be a cure.

My mother was once asked to take our gander to the home of Peggy Coolay, a neighbour who had a sick child on one of the lonely farms at Keownnafauil. She did so and the child must have recovered because when my mother got sick herself later on the Coolays came to visit her and gave great help both inside and outside of the house, saying they always remembered her kindness with the gander! I expect she must have looked like old Pad Bwee with the Highland pipes when she arrived to do her doctoring with a screeching gander under her arm! God pity the little child having to open its mouth so that a hissing gander with a snake-like neck might blow its breath into its throat! It was enough to frighten the life out of anyone not to mind a little child but I suppose it frightened away the germs of disease as well.

Jamesy O'Loughlin's father, Barney Thomaus, who was a great man for stories, told me that the swollen roots of the Mock-an-dhaw-how which look like parsnips or potatoes were often used by the old people to cure carbuncles which they believed were caused by an evil worm working its destruction on the flesh and that if he could be given a bad shock it would kill him and the sore would heal. This was done by placing the roasted root of the Mock-an-dhaw-how against the carbuncle, but the cure should be arranged out of the patient's hearing because he gets extra sensitive and cautious on account of the trouble. If he knew what was coming he would get afraid, the worm would learn of the danger in store for him and retire behind the scenes until the operation was over, then return with double the venom in revenge for the trick they tried to play on him. So the patient was sent out on some pretence or other for the time being, the roots put roasting on a pan and when all was ready the lot would be hidden and he would be called in again on some other excuse. Then, after some short general conversation he would be asked casually to let them see the carbuncle by way of no harm. When he did so the "doctor" would suddenly press the hot root to it and the great shock would kill the worm. If it did not kill the man as well he would make a quick recovery. The main hope lay in the quickness of the doctor and the slowness of the worm. If he got the slightest hint of the conspiracy he was gone west on them by the time the cure was ready. When he was dead and the wound opened, out came his ugly white body with legs and arms like an octopus. It had to be taken out in pieces and sometimes these looked so strange in shape that people said, "rags, bones and the devil knows what" came out of the wound, whispering also that they had been put there previously by the fairies when they found the patient out late and regarded him as a trespasser breaking their unwritten law which said that the day was for the living and the night was for the dead.

The Head Mistress of the girls' school had a big brown setter that wandered in and out of the school-yard whenever she pleased. Her name was Queeney. Somewhere in her wanderings she found poisoned food and that was the end of her. The Head Mistress was naturally upset for she believed that the poisoning was done intentionally. She spoke with great emotion about it to the girls, my sisters said, and comforted herself with a closing remark that "the Day of Judgment will tell who killed Queeney!" Most people in our valley who suffered wrongs for which they had no hope of redress in this world looked forward to that dreadful event for justice.

When the Head Mistress got married it meant a change in her name. The scholars had to give up calling her Miss Devlin and call her Mrs. O'Shannissey instead for her husband was a namesake of ours from near the Pond of the Water-lilies in Killarney. As they had no family some thoughtless people jibed about them behind their backs. One morning, after they had been married a few years, a namesake of theirs who had a little shop in Gurthagreenane met my three sisters on their way to school. He asked them where they were going. When they told him he said: "Go back home, my girls. You have no business in school to-day." They were puzzled, of course, and asked him the reason. "You aren't after hearing the news then?" he said, letting on to be surprised. "What news?" they asked, thinking that perhaps the school had fallen as I had often hoped it would. "The Mistress had twins last night!" he answered, walking away without as much as moving an eyelid.

We were having the summer holidays while I was still in the Second Class when we heard the sad news that the Assistant Master died after a short sickness. Everyone in the place was

78

sorry for him and his family who were very popular. The people praised him greatly, saying that he was a very jolly man in his time, full of harmless tricks that made his neighbours laugh. They also said that he played beautifully on the fiddle and had taught some of his daughters to play as well. After his death we still bought our pencils, pens and books from his wife who carried on the business as usual.

I was very shy about meeting shopkeepers or anyone I thought better off than we were at home. I thought their children were nicer-looking than country children. Their clean tidy dress added to their looks compared with the ragged clothes country children wore. Their parents I thought were the cream of society, though in reality they were only butchers, bakers, tailors, carpenters, blacksmiths, publicans and grocers.

Now and again in sleep I have a curious nightmare. I am on my way to school, walking up the middle of the village of Gurthagreenane. All the shopkeepers and their children stare at me and laugh. I look at myself to see what is wrong. Horror of horrors, I have come away from home without my trousers! I have nothing on me but a shirt. I open my mouth wide and take a long worried breath to relieve the tension. I turn and bolt from the crowd, my shirt growing shorter with every step I take. It seems to get right over my head as I sweep round the corner by the police barrack and there she sits by the window, Rachel O'Hara, the lovely daughter of the cross policeman, looking at me straight in the eye now that I do not want her to see me at all after looking the other way whenever I did! "Brian! Brian!" she shouts in the friendliest possible way. My own mother could not do it nicer. But Rachel dear, you call me at the wrong time. She persists. I am just in the act of jumping into a barrel of water standing beside the barrack, intending to hide myself and do my serenading from a cooler place with my head just over the top before jumping out again, borrowing a sheet Moll Tim has just hung out on the line, wrapping it round me and clearing for the hills when the "Brian! Brian!" starts again. Yes, it really does come from, no, not Rachel, but my mother, calling me to get up for school and warning me that if I don't I shall be late! I find myself in a great sweat. How could it be otherwise after coming out of a

79

barrel of water! I have kicked all the bedclothes out on the floor, leaving not a stitch on either myself or Murty. I jump out, put the clothes back on Murty, still sleeping soundly, and then dress myself quickly, being particularly careful not to forget my trousers!

IX

Ignorance

AFTER having been to school for a few years I noticed that nearly all the other boys were interested in cattle while I was not. I worried a good deal about this for I had heard people say that a farmer with no interest in animals would never get on in life. At that time the whole world seemed to be one vast collection of farms. How could I know any better? I had never seen a city or even a big town and the seventeen houses which surrounded the school were, I thought, the last word in communal life.

"That's a nice little heifer, God bless her," said Maurice O'Grady as we passed one grazing on the mountain on our way to school.

"What's the difference between her and any other heifer?" I ask.

"Don't you see the colour, man?" and he looks at me, surprised at either my ignorance or blindness.

"What difference does the colour make, Maurice?"

"Colour is it? God help your head, indeed. A strawberry heifer like her would take the eye of a jobber at any fair from here to Magherafelt," said the wise and knowing Maurice while I listened with my mouth open and wondered why I could not think as he did. "If she was white, you fool," he continued, "nobody would bother about her."

"Isn't a white cow as good as a strawberry one any day?" I ventured.

"Och, mu lowm, then, if that's all you know! A white cow is likely to have white calves, isn't she?"

"I don't know; and what's wrong with that anyhow?"

"There is no take for white cattle."

"Why is that?"

"It seems the quality of the meat in white animals is not so good as in others. Glory be to goodness, man, sure everyone knows that."

81

I did not, and I felt there was something wrong with me.

"How did you find out all this?" I asked, as I watched him walking smartly along, the weight of knowledge taking nothing from the lightness of his step.

"Find it out, is it?" he said with a comfortable easy laugh. "There was no finding out in it. I knew it since the first day I saw an animal. Sure I'm all my life listening to that sort of thing. My father was a jobber in his young days, do you see, and a man of money too, im breersa fain."

Then I remembered that I too had often heard my father and others talk about these things but that I had taken little notice of what they said because I was not interested in their conversation. They seemed to have the knowledge born with them. Instinct seemed to tell them everything useful and sensible in the walk of life in which God had placed them. I could never think as they did no matter how hard I tried. Their minds were always on the land and everything connected with it. They seemed to want nothing else, whereas my mind was always wandering towards the outside world and away from farming in general. I tried to concentrate on what everyone agreed was proper for a farmer's son but I could not. I wanted to be like others so that I could hold my own among them and I felt miserable thinking that there were many things of importance missing from my mind.

My mother had a poor knowledge of animals compared with my father who was considered very gifted in that respect, but she had a great interest in them, knowing that the family's welfare depended on them. When she found me so careless about them she looked on me with pity, shook her head and said: "God help us, Brian, my boy, I'm afraid you'll never make out in the world!"

After coming home from school I take my dinner and sit aimlessly on the settle thinking, ever thinking of the strangeness of the world. It is a summer evening and golden-tinted clouds rest peacefully above the deep blue mountains in the west where the sun has just gone down. The air is calm and silent except for the buzzing of an occasional beetle but suddenly the silence is broken by a loud and lonely baa-aa coming from the little field west of the hay-rick. My mother jumps up from her stool when she hears it. "The devil be from

82

us," she cries, "I forgot to feed the calves." She rushes about, her long wide flannel dress brushing the ground, pours milk from a pan into a big metal pot and hangs it over the fire. When it is heated a little she tests its temperature while stirring it about with her hand and then pours it into two buckets which she gives me to take to the calves. "Feed the two red ones first," she directs, "and beat the others away with the rod you'll find inside the gap. Then you can come back for the rest. Mind out now that they don't spill it on you. The big spotted fellow is the devil himself for pucking the bucket."

I take both buckets to the stone fence where the calves are assembled, their heads stretching over it and every one of them trying to bellow louder than his neighbour. After finding the rod I lift one of the buckets over the fence and allow only one calf to drink while I have to keep beating away the others until their turn comes. When he reaches the bottom he keeps on sucking at the zinc bucket until there is nothing more that he can drink. Then I beat him away also and take back the bucket. When the next calf is fed in the same way I take the empty buckets back to the house where my mother has a fresh supply ready for the two more. "Be sure to give the finger to the small calfeen," she warns me, "or he won't drink his share." That was a job I hated because I was afraid he might bite my fingers. I was too green to know that he had no teeth! "Damn him," says I, "if it isn't full of taspy he is!" Calves are like people; some of them are very queer. However I take the bucket to the fence and feed the small calfeen last with the height of coaxing and trouble. He keeps pucking the bucket. That is bad enough but I have the additional bother of beating away the others who come along licking their lips, sucking each other's ears and throwing their hind legs into the air as they face the bucket expecting a second helping as if I have nothing else to do but drawing milk to them and I having plenty lessons to learn that they know nothing about. Finally the little calf puts his head into the bucket but not into the milk for he persists in pucking the sides instead of doing the sensible thing— drinking the milk. At last I put my finger into his mouth and he starts sucking as if it is a sweet! What flaming fools these calves are! But I see my chance for getting him to drink. I lower my finger into the milk and, while his main object is to

83

suck, he drinks at the same time. I can assure you that I feel glad when he reaches the bottom. I lift my finger and his head follows it out of the bucket which I remove quickly and, taking a parting glance at the clouds which are now no longer golden but grey and lonesome-looking, I take the buckets back to the house and hope that I won't get the job of "giving the finger" to that little nuisance for a while again.

Silly ass, or calf I should say! and yet for all that I was like him myself because I needed a lot of petting before I would do what was expected of me. While everyone else went directly to business I was always trying to reach the same point by an indirect route to suit the quaintness of my views as people often told me and losing thereby many of the good things the others seemed to gain. While I disliked feeding calves or having anything to do with animals and tried to avoid the jobs as much as possible, the neighbouring boys would be deeply interested in them and would volunteer where I would shirk. In addition to this they would keep a close watch on the growth of all animals and feel as pleased as could be when they saw them "coming on and putting up meat." Heaven only knows how many other things they noticed which escaped my attention completely and which are still far beyond my knowledge.

My father was naturally disappointed to find me like this and he too thought I would never get on in the world. He would often lose his temper with me and call me nasty names because I failed to see or do the obvious thing even when he directed me where to see and how to do it. Small blame to the poor man for asking himself why I was not like every other boy in the place.

I was worried about the situation myself for I felt I was destined to be a failure in life. To add to my troubles I was not good-looking like my sisters who were admired by everyone, or Murty who was "the picture of his father." Some of the neighbours made no secret of their dislike for me on account of my looks. When they praised the others they did not forget to pass the opposite remarks about me to balance things. This gave me the impression that no one would ever want me in life and it had a very depressing effect on me. My parents were both handsome and had the world of respect for good-looking people but were inclined to think poorly of the plain no matter what other good qualities they had.

When I went down the fields and called to the house of our cousin Kate O'Mahoney she would give me a big piece of bread and butter and sometimes make me sit down to dinner with her family. My sisters and I were always warned by our parents not to be calling to the houses of the neighbours. "Cadging and cabin-hunting" my father called it when he wanted to stop us, but we often disregarded his warnings and enjoyed the good things which the generous neighbours gave us.

"Have ye many cows calved?" Kate would ask as she placed a big cup of new milk before me.

"I don't know," I would truthfully answer, and that was a terrible admission of ignorance for a farmer's son to make, moreover when his people had only five cows altogether!

Kate would only have asked the question to find out if we had enough milk at home so that she might send us some if we had not, as she had often done before. But I did not understand that unless the cows had calved there could be no milk from them.

My meals at home were put before me each day as if they had fallen from heaven. I never stopped to ask where they came from or by what means they had arrived. I was a devil-may-care in that respect. But that would never do on a farm.

What wonder was it then that in the course of time people began to look upon me as a softie without any sense. Whenever they felt like asking a question about anything, they passed me by as if I did not exist, and went on to consult one of the clever fellows who was supposed to know all the answers. If they did not know it and I did, there was no use in my going up and saying it, for I was a boy of straw in everybody's eyes.

To add to my embarrassment, as if I had not enough trouble already, what do you think of my devil of a Nelly O'Grady, but to start letting on that she and I were courting in the quiet! She was a sister to Maurice and was a few years older than both of us. On the way home from school she would run up beside me, put her arm about me and kiss me before I knew where I was. The others would burst out laughing when they saw me blush like a burning bush and I would not hear the end of their jeers for a week after. The boys would tell each other about it and make fun of me whenever they got the chance. I was tormented so much in this way as well as in others that I hated the sight of boys in general.

In these troubles it was only natural that I should seek the protection of my sisters because my tormentors were afraid to interfere with me when they were present. That only started a new problem, because going about with my sisters made it necessary for me to take part in the girls' games which I did gladly because I was no use at those played by the boys, such as marbles, burling and football. The girls had a game called "Highgates" and I enjoyed that as well as one called "Thread, thread the needle, O." In both these games one party would march under arches made by another holding hands. But there was a special game that I hated like rank poison because I was sure to be made the principal fool in it with all the others laughing at me. The name of it was "My Dilsee-dolsee dee" and it gave Nelly her great chance for making a public show of me. You may be sure she made a field-day out of it. How I hated her little black head as she went around supervising the game. I stood among the girls innocently hoping that I might be lucky enough to escape her eagle eye and never suspecting that she was getting up the game specially to catch me. A ring would be formed with all of us holding hands around someone who had to stand in the middle. Everyone would start to dance, the circle narrowing and widening as they moved in and out in waves of excitement, singing verses which ended with "My Dilsee-dolsee dee" until they came to the part which directed the person in the middle to pick a partner from the circle:

"Now go 'round and choose your own,
And choose your own, and choose your own,
Now go 'round and choose your own,
My Dilsee-dolsee dee."

The chooser would then take a partner into the middle and wait for the verse which directed them to kiss. All went well for me until it came to Nellie's turn to stay in the middle and then my fate was sealed. No sooner had the verse began which told her to do the choosing than she would spring at me like a cat, accompanied by roars of laughter from the others when they saw my cheeks glowing with embarrassment, and there, in

86

front of my sisters and everyone else, she would kiss me shamelessly!

Upon my soul it was bad enough being hunted by O'Grady's gander but it was ten times worse being hunted by O'Grady's daughter! The gander's hisses were at least genuine but Nellie's kisses were not. If she was anything like Rachel O'Hara itself things might not have been so bad and a pleasant chance might take the place of a horrible fix but there was nothing of the Juliet in Nellie and less of the Romeo in me!

X

A Narrow Escape

WHILE my grandmother kept us in constant touch with the next world she did not forget to tell us about the grim link that joined it with this. That link was Death. We asked her what it was like. She said it came in the shape of a little black man who stole into people's beds and choked them. I can see him now as I pictured him then: small, black-skinned, with very white teeth exposed in a grinning mouth, always standing outside my bed in deep mourning, waiting a chance to get at me. Around his neck he wore a tight-fitting white Eton collar to go with his teeth as well as being a symbol of his trade in the chokery business. It surprised me that my grandmother was not afraid of him at all. She was not even afraid to die. I was very much so myself, on account of the smothering I expected to get in the grave. The result of the little black man's visit, and a future of misery in the cold, damp, silent clay, where one must lie a hopeless prisoner till the end of time, seemed a horrible change from the sweet comfort of being alive in a bright and cheerful world.

I had seen a dead body only once. That was when my grandfather died, God rest him, but as I was then only three years old I had only a hazy recollection of the event. I remember that when he was alive he had a long sharp kind-looking face. He took me by the hand to walk about the yard in the early summer. We listened to the corncrake and in imitation of that queer bird he repeated "Ceeok, caiok; ceeok, caiok," for my amusement. Of all he said these words alone remained in my memory. I was about two and a half years old at the time. When his last hour came we all knelt beside his bed to pray for his soul which was then about to depart. Kate O'Mahoney, his first cousin, was there. She shut his eyes and mouth after he was dead. His body was laid out on the settle under a canopy of white sheets. My grandmother told me to kiss his cold white face as she lifted me in her arms and took me over to see him. After that he seemed to have got lost in the crowd coming to his wake and funeral and I do not remember seeing him any more.

After he was buried, however, my grandmother did not allow us to forget him. She taught us to say "The Lord have mercy on his soul" every night and morning as well as to say special prayers for him and for all the dead in the months of October and November, moreover on All Souls' Night when she said they would be likely to return to this world in search of friends who might be willing to plead for their release from Purgatory. She had asked my grandfather before he died if he would like to come back. He said he would of course but he never seemed to be able to do so.

It was the custom for each old woman to have her habit or funeral shroud always ready in case she dropped off suddenly. It was a long brown garment of standard make, somewhat like that worn by the Franciscans. The letters "I H S" were embroidered on the breastpiece which the country people took to mean "I have suffered" but which were really a symbol of Our Lord.

My grandmother bought the cloth for her habit in Gurthagreenane and got it made to measure by Alice the dressmaker. A brown cap, gloves and stockings went with it. When she had it made Alice saw my grandmother coming towards the shop and hurried into it, met her at the door and asked her was it a good fit! She retired quickly, however, for she expected a good telling-off. Then she parcelled it up for my grandmother who took it home and laid it away carefully until the time of need.

"I will wear that hereafter," she would say as she took it out of her box to air it in the summer. "It will quench the fire of hell for me."

I kept rolling the word "hereafter" over and over in my mind for it seemed to have great power over life and death. I fancied the fires quenching about her in all directions if my grandmother paid a courtesy visit to the lower regions later on. But in spite of all its power in the next world she was careful in spreading it out to air on the bushes not to leave it within a donkey's roar of the calves who were worse than the devil himself for chewing any cloth they could get hold of whether it belonged to this world or to the next!

While it was airing I looked at it with awe and fear but my grandmother seemed to feel proud of it. She took it carefully off the fence when it was aired, folded it neatly with the cap, gloves and stockings, put it back into the box and then we would soon forget all about it. But suddenly some neighbour would get sick and die without having made any preparations and as all the neighbours knew about my grandmother's care in that respect they would come to her in their trouble and ask her to be good enough to give them her habit to cover their dead, telling her they would have it replaced by another as soon as possible after the funeral. She always let them have it of course because everyone in the valley will do all they can to comfort each other in death or sickness, but I often heard her grumble about the poor quality of the habit she got in return for the one of good material which had given her so much trouble in choosing at the shop and preserving so carefully for such a long time. She had paid dearly for the best she could find so that it might look respectable when her corpse would be laid out and people would come from far and near to her wake and funeral. She knew the old women would stand over her, examine the habit from head to foot and even feel the material between their fingers to test its quality. "Handling the habit" was a well-known custom with them. How could my grandmother bear to hear them say as they nudged each other in the sly: "Och, an' sure 'tis only an old rag!" and she not able to answer back, give an explanation or tell them to mind their own business as she might have done had she been alive! That, and the fact that she would have to wear it for the rest of her life after dying was enough to make her turn in her grave before going into it at all!

Alas; one by one the neighbours passed away in their turn and it was not always the old who died either. Poor Paddy MacNamara, Kate O'Mahoney's only son, was only six months married when he got rheumatic fever after getting a bad wetting when taking pigs to the fair of Ballyvourney across the mountains and in spite of everything being done for him he died on a late September morning when the harvesting was over. I remember two of the neighbouring boys coming to our house for the habit to put on him. His death put a great gloom on the whole parish because he was so young and his people were very highly thought of. I heard the ullagoaning of his relatives when his coffin was taken out of the house and brought along the rough bohereen on the shoulders of his neighbours until they reached the main road which was black with people waiting to convey him to the grave. He was not buried long either when a report went out that Nancy Taid had heard him calling her in the dead hour of the night and that she had answered him. She got sick right away. When my mother called to see her she said that if she had her time over again she would not answer, even though the man calling from the other world was her own cousin itself. It is believed that if a person called is foolish enough to answer in a case like that either he or she must go to the caller by dying soon after. That was the case with Nancy Taid. She died six months after Paddy. Her death was not expected so soon and again my grandmother's habit was sent for to put on her. The wailing of her family was something terrible when she was taken out of the house never to return and for the first time in my life I learned to pity her daughter Nellie and to forget the way she had tormented me.

Many other neighbours came for my grandmother's habit in the same way and only in one case did the very one she had lent come back unworn by the dead. In all the other cases, alas, it went directly to the grave but now it was given an unexpected reprieve and a further chance of airing! That was a bad omen for herself, by the way, but we did not notice it at the time. They say that supplying coffins is an unlucky trade and maybe supplying habits is the same. Leaving that on the clevvy, however, here is what happened:

Another young man with three children who lived near O'Mahoney's Gullet got a bad fit of sickness and lay in bed for a long time. He was attended by the doctor who finally gave up all hope for his recovery. His name was Darby O'Keefe and his wife was a cousin of ours through the O'Mahoneys. All the neighbours were full of sympathy for him and for his family. He was an only son too and people say that these are always unlucky. He had a terrible sore leg and the old women said that a lot of rags, bones and other old rubbish had come from the wound. They sent for the priest of course and he prepared him for the next world because he too had no hope for him in this. Everyone had given him up for a lost case; everyone, indeed, except Darby himself! Strangely enough he knew that he was not to die as soon as the others expected. His hopes lay partly on the fact that he had not heard "The Modhereeneey Gheeve," a pack of hounds from the other world, the Lord save us, that come howling to the door at night whenever any of his family is to die. He could not say what was in his mind for he was speechless and without power in any way except that he could still draw a few faint breaths to keep the life in him.

I remember the time well. It was Saint Stephen's Night and people were saying that if he died within the twelve days of Christmas he would be sure to go to heaven. The Litany for the Dying was read over him and all the prayers his relatives and friends could think of were offered up for the safety of his soul on its journey to the stars. Nell O'Mahoney, his mother-in-law, was stooping over him trying to shut his eyes and mouth but they would not stay as she wanted them. She squeezed his nostrils, an old custom, to prevent the worms from going into them after he was buried. While she was doing these things his brother-in-law was busy with a hammer in the kitchen driving nails into the joists overhead so as to hang up the sheets which were to form a canopy over the corpse when it would be laid on the settle. Darby's father was sent with a neighbour for my grandmother's habit. He arrived in the middle of the night, poor man, and he was a sorrowful sight. By the light of the Christmas candle I could see the tears falling from his red eyes as he wiped his long white wrinkled face with a handkerchief. He looked weary and desolate but that was no wonder after all the sleepless nights and days he had of watching over the sick. It was quite normal for a young man to go for the habit for his father but here it was the father coming for it for his son. My grandmother found the precious habit, parcelled it up and gave it to him with a prayer for the dead. I remember his drooping figure as he went out into the gloom with the mournful bundle under his arm and words of sympathy going with him from my father, mother and grandmother, for his case was pitiful indeed.

Meantime preparations for the wake were going on in

Darby's home but when old Nell found that his eyes would not shut properly she began to complain under her breath because there is a belief that when this happens there will soon be another death in the family as the corpse is only trying to keep an eye open for a companion in the grave! Some calm and thoughtful neighbour present said that, maybe, after all, the preparations were a little in advance of the event occasioning them so she asked the man with the hammer to stop his work for a little while. "Stop it, is it?" said he with a frown as he picked up another nail. "Sure, woman dear, 'tis no time to be doing it when the corpse is cold!" In our valley people make it a point to have the corpse laid out as soon as possible so that the hands and feet may be put into proper positions before the stiffness of death sets in and the neighbours gather about it for the wake.

Nell had succeeded in keeping Darby's mouth shut in a fairly respectable way by putting a prayer book under his jaw. She had given up fiddling with his nose when someone suggested a little glue for the eyes. Nobody present knew where the glue was only Darby himself and he was afraid of his life that they might find it. When he thought they were hot on the scent he made an effort to mislead them by trying to tell them it was behind the horse on a shelf in the stable. The same horse would kick the stars for nothing and Darby knew well that nobody there that night would dare to enter the stable if his eyes stayed as open as The Gap of Dunloe. But Darby's voice was gone. He made one final effort, however. The valves in his throat opened suddenly at the word "stable." That came out with such sudden violence that Nell drew back and went near breaking her head on the room-door behind her. It startled everyone in the house and put a hasty stop to their gallop. When they got over the shock they soon found that the man was not dead at all. They took the prayer book from under his chin and instead of hindering his breathing they tried to help it. The high tension came down. Everyone got quiet and it was not long before Darby began to talk in faint whispers. By the time his father arrived with the habit he was able to take a little drink from a spoon held gently by the same Nell who a short time before was looking for the glue, because she was really a generous good-natured woman misguided in her zeal for carrying out old customs to the letter.

From that onwards Darby made a rapid recovery which surprised the whole parish. We had all expected his wake and funeral as much as Nell and the others. Sure, more power to his windpipe, my Darby is living still! "It was a hard thing to find them holding my nose," I heard him say later, "when I couldn't lift a hand to stop them, and I wanted all the breathing I had at the time. Ah, yes then; hard is no name for it, indeed; and while they were nailing up the sheets you may be sure that every sound of the hammer went through my head and not a word could I say against it."

He was up and around again by the time the habit was returned to my grandmother and everyone in the place was rejoicing at what they called "The Resurrection of Darby O'Keefe."

News of a death would spread quickly. People from all over the parish would flock to the wake. Sometimes to satisfy the craving of certain people for news some playboy like Pat Mulloy of Coomlaegill would tell them of the death of someone at the far end of the valley. "Wisha, the poor woman, God help her," one would say, "wasn't it quick she went after all!" and the story would spread. Other women would believe it, get ready and go off towards the "wake" with their black shawls over their heads, only to be stopped on the way and told it was a hoax. The people whose relative was said to be dead would naturally resent it and swear hell for leather against the person who first told the story but you can't stop the mouth of a liar. My grandfather had a cousin called Tim Dinneen who wandered from place to place working for farmers. He had no home of his own, poor fellow, and a report went out that he had died in Ballyvourney, the next parish to ours. It was taken for a fact by everyone in our valley. Tim was indignant, of course, when he came around Gurthagreenane once more and was told the news. Either to drown his sorrow or to celebrate the fact that he was still alive in spite of reports to the contrary he got pasted drunk in the village but by a strange irony when the public houses were shut he went into the graveyard to sleep with the dead for want of accommodation with the living. When he woke up in the morning and found where he was his anger returned. "It was bad enough," he said, "being dead in Ballyvourney and getting out of it but, my corpse from the devil, 'tis nearly as bad to find myself alive in the graveyard here without knowing from Adam how I got into it!" He was still suffering from the effects of the drink and it did not improve matters when he found a half-pint of whiskey in his pocket and drank it. Most people put on their clothes when they get up in the morning but Tim reversed the order by taking off every stitch he had on him and standing on the wall of the graveyard over-looking the main street of Gurtha-greenane. He started ullagoaning and when the people looked out of their windows there was my Tim as naked as Adam on the wall, shouting at the top of his voice: "Here is Tim Dinneen that died in Ballyvourney!"

XI

Storms and Troubles

THE Parish of Gurthagreenane is in the wettest part of Ireland. The rain comes in torrents and keeps falling for weeks at a time. On that account the farmers often find it hard to save their crops, especially hay and oats. They must rush about if they get a few dry days by chance so as to save as much as they can before the rain returns. Sometimes the fog rolls over the mountains, then settles on them like a cape. When it gets like that on certain hills the wise farmers say it is a sure sign of rain, which comes anyhow, cape or no cape.

My father has a big field of hay cut down and nearly saved. It lies in little grass-cocks, looking like warts on the field. We are all out early with our croppy pikes helping him to shake it out in the sun which is shining brightly in the east. We work hard for if we can get it dried before the rain comes it can be drawn into the yard, stored in the new hay-shed and our trouble with it will be over.

When it is all shaken out my father sends me around to ask some of the neighbouring men to help us to lift up a sick cow in the crow. Dansel O'Kaine, Pat Mulloy and Michael O'Grady come along and suggest remedies for her; a drink of bran-water, a nice hot mess of boiled potatoes and Indian meal mixed with a pinch of saltpetre, a dose of castor oil, and so on. They push pieces of sacking underneath and lift her to her shaky feet, watching her carefully as she steadies herself slowly. Nobody knows what is wrong with her. My father has been very lucky with the cattle up to now. "I hadn't a sick cow in the place since my father died, God rest him," he tells the others as they talk about her. But they can't afford to delay long for they all have hay to look after as well as us. "The Lord spare you all the health," my father calls after them as they turn to go home.

When we return to the field my father lights his pipe with an ominous look in his eyes as he turns them towards the western sky.

"I'm afraid of it," he says, taking up his pike. " 'Tis getting dark over the bay but with God's help it may stay dry till we finish. There is a little black cap on Filemore too and I don't like that."

Meantime the sun shines gloriously all over the valley. Bees hum about us in all directions and the fragrant smell of honey and flowers is filling the air. We all get busy, turn over the hay and then go in to dinner. After that my father brings the horse and cart into the field and we help him to fill the load. When it is full he secures it with ropes, takes it up into the yard and empties it into the shed. Bridget, Eileen and I get busy collecting more hay into long winding heaps called "lhaurhawns" to have it convenient for filling into the next load. But just as my father brings the horse and cart along again we feel a few stray drops of rain strike our faces. The wind grows a little stronger. We see a small shower sprinkling the hills across the valley. We work harder and still harder to get the hay together and save as much as we can by making it into cocks as we have now given up the idea of taking any more into the shed except the load my father is already taking there. I go with him in frantic haste to get the contents of the load into the shed and when that is done we return to the field. But the rain is too quick for us. It sweeps along in our direction. Down it comes and before we know where we are the whole field is drenched. We go back home and most of our hard day's work is gone for nothing.

When we arrive in the yard my father untackles the horse and puts him into the stable where he gets very uneasy through fear of the loud noise made by the heavy rain pounding on the zinc roof. He lifts his head in fright every time a fresh gust of wind makes the noise still louder. It pours and pours for hours without stopping. We watch it through the window of the kitchen. A constant stream is falling from the thatch and big floods are tearing up red furrows in the ground. I don't know how it is, but I always delight in floods. They make waterfalls and great pools in unexpected places among the rocks and fences.

When it lightens a little I put an old sack over my shoulders and take a stroll to see the wonders of the waters. The Coomlaegill river has widened out to twenty times its normal size. It spreads along the foot of the valley like a long yellowish-white lake winding this way and that as it roars along to the sea. White streams are showing on the dark faces of the blue hills like great human tears which I can see plainly now that the rain has stopped completely. These streams rush down to bigger ones, these in turn to still bigger; the whole lot going headlong in wild fury over old and new courses to the great winding rolling river below. It is a scene never to be forgotten.

Sometimes these rains would start on market days and catch people out who could not reach their homes on account of the flooded fords on many of the by-roads which had no bridges. The winds roared through the valley lifting the roofs from houses and knocking down great trees. Some people would stop the roofs from lifting by throwing ropes across them with the ends tied to cart-wheels or other heavy articles to weigh them down. It was often I sat comfortably by the fire listening to the great "boo-oo-oo" as the wind blew over the top of the chimney in these storms. My grandmother's three nephews were married in Slievelea, the next townland to ours on the County Cork side. They had two dangerous fords to cross on their way to and from Gurthagreenane village. When they got caught in a storm they would flock into our house with their friends, take off their wet coats and sit by the fire until the floods went down. If it was dark by then they would pour paraffin oil on dry sods of turf stuck on the pointed ends of sticks to be lighted when they reached the fords so that they might see the stepping-stones.

These storms would often last for days and nights without stopping, then finish up suddenly. In a short time the sun would be out again. The country would then look its best. Towards evening the hills would put on their lovely deep blue and the sky its golden red. No matter where we turned our eyes we could see nothing but a scene of beauty in the fields and woods and mountains. Oh, that lovely valley! And the dear old cabin lying among the grey rocks that gave it shelter. I see it always in my fondest dreams, for ever cherished in the memories of childhood, more loved than all the gaudy castles that the hand of man could raise.

The great storms had a double fury in winter. The wind

swept along the valley with a mighty frightening force. I was often caught in it on my way home from school. I would soon be drenched into the skin. I could smell the soot and smoke of the old house as the water ran from my cap in streams about my face. At night my father and mother would be in great dread lest the wind should blow the roof from the house. Sometimes I secretly hoped that it would for I should like to see what it might look like without it. I thought of how nice it would be to climb the ladder to the loft and find the roof gone. Then when the rain would be over I could remove a few loose boards from the loft, sit beside the fire, look up at the stars and wonder what they were doing! It was to save them from these mighty winds that people always built their houses in sheltered nooks instead of in open spaces.

It rains and blows in various ways for the most part of nine months each year in our valley. But now and again, the weather is so freaky, that we may have two lovely dry months following each other, while next year the same months may be wet and dreary from end to end. We can never trust the weather in Ireland. On that account the farmers have a hard time because sometimes they wait in vain for even one fine week in which to save their crops. If they do not get it the hay and corn are left to rot in the fields. If they are lucky the weather will suddenly change from wet to dry and remain that way until long after all the crops are saved.

I got so used to the rain that I took but little notice of it. In fact I grumbled that it did not come oftener, especially in the mornings, so that I might not have to go to school, where I hated going, wet or dry. I remember many a morning lying awake in bed, praying fervently to God and Saint Patrick to send it down in torrents, for then my mother would say: "Brian, my boy, you needn't get up for a while. Stay where you are, out of the way. 'Tis too wet to go to school. 'Tis pouring down from the heavens." That sounded sweeter than the Harps of Tara. My heart would leap for joy. I would cover my head with the blankets and a prayer of thanks would rise to heaven for opening its flood-gates in the hour of need! I had the faith of the world in Saint Patrick for remembering me on these mornings. He treated me well, God bless him. It often left off raining when the time for going to school was past. Then I would have a fine day to roam the hills in freedom. When I went to Mass on Saint Patrick's Day it was no wonder that I felt thrilled when the Head Master's wife played the lovely soft-toned harmonium as the choir sang:

"All praise to Saint Patrick who brought to our mountains
The gift of God's faith, the sweet light of His love,"

for indeed I felt that he had brought lots of other things as well. And when they had finished singing about the memories of "hundreds of years through smiles and through tears" that "come back to us every Saint Patrick's Day" my soul was lifted to the heavens with delight at the idea of this great and holy man being so attentive to my prayers!

The sick cow recovered for the time being but a few weeks later she got struck again and died. My father and mother were very upset and so was my grandmother who was then confined to her bed for some time. When I went into the room to tell her she sighed and said: "Dear God bless the creature for she was the nice kind little cow and 'twas many a gallon of milk she gave us, my sorrow for her." I watched my father dig a grave for her in a lonely corner of a field a good way from the house. Barney O'Loughlin's wife, Nellie Matt, warned him not to bury her in the same grave as any of the cows which had died before because she said it was an unlucky thing to do, and that it might mean the death of another animal. The same men who helped to lift her up the day we were at the hay now came to take her from the crow to the grave. I saw my mother cry in the yard as they did so. "Starry" was her name and we were all very lonesome after her. My grandmother closed her eyes and shook her head as she lay in bed. "God help us," she said, "I'll soon go myself as well as her, for I haven't much strength left in me now and I'm afraid March will carry me." That was the month all the old people feared on account of its harsh winds but as my own blood was hot I never noticed them blowing in all their bitterness.

XII

Wandering Visitors

IT was a lovely Saturday evening in early August, corn
ripening in the fields, potatoes blossoming in the gardens
and gentle breezes moving the leaves about. Looking out
I saw Pat Mulloy coming down The Rock in his grey
bauneen and flannel trousers, his hob-nailed boots making a
great rattle like the clatter of a horse's hooves as he strolled
carelessly along lilting to himself:

"Hie, dee-idle-ee, dilla-dee-idle-ee,
Dally-dil-owdle-il-idle-ee-dee."

He walked into the kitchen with an air of great unconcern as
if he was living with us and was only just coming in to light
his pipe. He went up silently and stood for a few seconds with
his back to the fire.

"Well, Pat, my boy," said my mother, looking up from her
sewing, "have you any news?"

"Devil carry the word."

"Why then, that's seldom with you; but sure they say no
news is good news. 'Tis a grand day outside, thank God, for
anyone walking about."

"It is, indeed," and Pat moved towards my sister Abbey who
was pouting over something in the corner, "and a fine day too
for a girl to be inside getting A B C on her shins."

"Mind your own business, Patcheen," said Abbey with a
nasty frown, for she was very cranky at the time and Pat was
only raising her temper for fun.

He stooped down, looked closer at her and drew his hands
through her hair. "Holy Brendan!" he cried in feigned surprise. "That child is ate alive with lice!"

We all laughed loudly. That made Abbey worse. She reached
for the tongs to hit him but we stopped her. She soon calmed
down and made friends with him only to be roused again by
some other nasty remark, for Pat always took delight in teasing
cranky people.

"Go away home and mind your hungry old jennet," said Abbey with a sneer. "It will pay you better than wandering about."

"Hoa, hu, hu! Hoa, hu, hu!" laughed Pat, thinking of some new prank.

"You can laugh now, indeed," said Abbey, "and maybe your own bed is worse than my head with fleas and boodies."

"Och, mu lhowm, they can't get into my bed," said Pat, taking a school-book from the table where Eileen had left it after looking over her lessons. "I shook lime around the khnasta to burn their knees and keep them out."

"You did in your hat," said Abbey, laughing. "I don't have to use either lime or pepper on my bed for there isn't a single flea or louse in it."

"Of course there isn't, for they're all married and have big families!"

He hummed a tune as he turned over the pages of the book until he came to "The Irish Emigrant's Lament" which he read out slowly and with great emotion. He made us all feel the same. But who can know the mind of a playboy? When he came to the words "I'll not forget you, darling, in the land I'm going to," he shut the book with a bang and flung it back on the table. "Hoa, hu, hu! Hoa, hu, hu!" he laughed, putting his hand into his waistcoat pocket and taking out his pipe. "I'll not forget you, darling! Hoa, hu, hu! The blarney galore that's in him! Darling, indeed, how are you! And the bloody bastard got married three times after going over!"

My youngest brother, Killian, was now about three years old. Pat turned to him and offered him a smoke. He put the pipe into his mouth but spat out quickly after doing so for it seems nobody likes tobacco the first time they taste it.

Pat had a nice little farm but as he lived alone he got tired of working and started wandering from house to house, always trying to have fresh news for his visits—news I am sorry to say that nobody believed for they knew it was only invented by him to suit the occasion.

When he was a boy he did not like going to school any more than I did so he did a lot of scheming to avoid it, spending many a day in an unoccupied house across the valley from the school. There he would light a fire and make himself comfortable. Curney O'Shea, the Head Master, would see the smoke and say to the other boys: "Ha, Pat has a bonfire again to-day," for he knew well who was there.

He was a fright to the world too for stealing fruit and he was always wandering like myself from bush to bush and from orchard to orchard. When one neighbour said "The green fruit will kill him," another laughed and said: "Don't worry. There is no fruit too green for Pat Mulloy."

In the middle of his conversation we heard the sound of foot-steps. It was Dannie O'Driscoll, the tinker, a great favourite in our house. He was a lanky young fellow wearing a foxy beard, closely trimmed with the shears, and he carried a black shiny leather budget on his back.

"Wisha, welcome, Dannie, my boy," said my mother when he came in and laid the budget on the floor.

"Thank you, ma'am," said Dannie.

"Sit down there for yourself till I make you a cup of tea," said my mother, wiping the dust from a chair with the corner of her sack-apron.

"The Lord spare you, ma'am," said Dannie, "and if I may be bold enough to ask, may I stay for the night, if you please?"

"You may, indeed, and welcome," said my mother, always kind to travellers, saying that nobody ever knew when their own would be on the road.

She stirred up the fire, added fresh turf to it and gave me a bucket to bring spring water from O'Grady's Well for the tea.

"Wait, Brian, and I'll be with you," said Pat who had kept silent since the tinker came in, and out he went as careless as ever, the hat thrown back on his poll at a rakish angle but a serious look on his face as he walked along like a trained soldier, singing: "When Sarsfield sailed away I wept when I heard the loud ochone." We parted at the foot of The Rock where he turned east towards the next house and I ran off to the well.

When I returned with the water my mother poured some into the kettle and hung it over the fire which was burning brightly. She laid the table and took down the tea-box from the clevvy.

"I have plenty tea of my own," said Danny, for he was after collecting it as he went about from house to house, "and plenty bread as well, thank God."

"The Lord keep plenty with you always."

He took a greyish-black tin from his pocket and handed it to her. "That's the tea," he said, and then he pulled some pieces of bread from the other pockets and laid them on the table.

When everything was ready and my mother had put some butter on the dish before him, he sat down to his meal and ate heartily. When he had finished he turned his chair about and told my mother the news he had gathered on his travels. He asked if she wanted any tin vessels mended. She said she did and, going up to the loft, she brought down a leaking bucket and a few saucepans she had put aside for his coming.

When he started to work it was a special joy for us to see him open the budget which, like my grandmother's box, seemed full of wonders. He selected his tools and began to work. He had a big scissors for cutting tin and it always attracted me so much on previous occasions that for weeks after he had left I used to try my mother's scissors on every old saucepan I could lay hands on in imitation of the clever work I had seen Dannie O'Driscoll do. It was only when my mother wanted to cut cloth later on that I would pay for my pleasure in lectures and stern warnings to let her scissors alone in the future. My brother Murty was also fascinated by the tinker's art and went so far as to ask my father to buy him a hundred-weight of tin to practise on!

"Where is the old woman?" asked Dannie, raising his head from his work, for he missed my grandmother who used to give shelter to him and his mother in the past.

"She's keeping the bed for the past few months, God help her," said my mother with a glance to the room-door. "She's old now, you know. She's well over the seventy-four."

"I'm sorry to hear that she's not well," said Dannie, putting down his hammer. "Will the noise bother her?"

"It won't indeed, my boy, for she's very deaf. But she has her senses as good as ever, thank God, and that's a great thing for a woman of her age."

My grandmother had been very kind to all of us and on that account we were always ready to answer her call when she wanted help. Every evening when I returned from school the first thing I did was to go to the room, kiss her and ask how she was getting on. Now and again I played harmless tricks on her but she never minded for she knew well that at the back of it all I was well disposed towards her.

My sisters and brothers crowded around Dannie as he went on with his work. I noticed that he had the mark of a very deep wound in the first finger of his left hand. It was healed up, of course, but a hollow appeared at each side as if a great nail had been driven through it. I wondered if he had had it done for some special purpose as the women do for putting rings in their ears! We asked him for the name of each tool. He told us, for he was always nice. The budget had a special interest for us apart from its use for holding tools. We had often heard it said that when tinkers got married they never went near the priest because that would cost too much money. When a couple wanted to roam the roads together they simply laid the budget on the ground and jumped over it. That was their form of marriage. "Jumping the Budget" was a common saying in our valley when referring to a tinker's wedding.

When Dannie had his work done he collected his tools, put them into the budget and sat down to converse with my father who had just come in. They talked mostly about fairs for Dannie had been to a good many in his time. He often brought news from Annaweelogue about people my mother knew and that made him extra welcome in our house. Sometimes the neighbours would come in and join the talk so that we would have a very pleasant time listening to them all.

When it was time for bed my father went out and brought in a big armful of hay which he laid on the floor.

"There now, Dannie, my boy," he said, "you can make yourself comfortable for the night."

When the neighbours had left my mother went up to the loft and brought down a few old blankets and quilts. Laying them on the hay she turned to Dannie and said: "You may lie on the settle or the floor whichever you like."

"I'll stay on the floor," said Dannie, putting his chair aside. "I'll have more room there to twist and turn without fear of falling."

We watched him spread the hay on the floor and when he had placed the blankets and quilts on it we all went to our beds and left him there folding his jacket neatly to act as a pillow. He always slept with his feet to the fire and his head to the doors as do most of these people.

As I lay in bed that night I thought of the story I had heard about a beggarman Darby O'Keefe's uncle kept of a time. He was sleeping in the same position as Dannie in the morning while the people of the house were out milking the cows. They forgot to shut the door. There was a cow loose in the yard and when she saw the hay on the floor she came in quietly and began to eat it. The beggarman was snoozing peacefully when she swept a bunch of his long hair into her mouth with the hay. Holy Patrick! Thousand murders! It was then the hullabaloo started, and by the luck of goodness Darby's uncle heard it and saved the poor man from a dreadful haircut!

When morning came Dannie took his breakfast by himself in the kitchen, my mother giving him fresh milk for his tea and any food he wanted. When he had finished he thanked us, took up his budget and went off whistling to the next house to see if they wanted any mending done.

There was usually a long stretch between Dannie's visits but this time to our surprise he returned within a week bringing a young woman with him. She was his wife, he told us, and a double bed had to be made for them that night. I was very anxious to ask, with my usual curiosity, if the budget he had with him was the one they had jumped over, but my mother warned me to keep my mouth shut, so I never found out.

Tinkers like Dannie were well liked. They never stole anything and were always willing to work for their keep. Each farmer had a particular tinker for doing his mending of pots and pans. Some tinkers took their families and belongings about with them in donkey-carts. They also took droves of donkeys for sale or exchange at fairs and so forth. In fact the donkey was so much identified with the tinker that whenever any of these despised animals was heard braying in the distance the country people stopped their work in the fields and said: "Whisht, you devil, you! There's a tinker dead somewhere!" That gave the impression that donkeys always mourned when friendless tinkers died!

Another favourite of ours was Daniel Courtney. He was not a tinker but "a travelling man" as we called beggars of his type. He was a very respectable old man in his ways and seemed to

106

be a person with whom the world had gone wrong in some way or another. He spoke gently to everyone, old and young.

Hearing the dog bark we ran to the door. It was Daniel.

"Good evening to you, woman of the house," he said to my mother as he walked in slowly, swinging an old sack of goods from his shoulder and laying it on the middle of the floor after the style of all these people.

"Yerra, how are you, Daniel?" said my mother, wiping the dust from the end of the settle for him to sit down; for the same dust was always flying about from the peat fire which had to be added to so often and the light ashes moved aside into the corner.

"Wisha, lhae, woman dear, I'm getting old," said he, sitting on the settle. "I can't get about as I did in the past. The bones are playing on me now, God help us."

"Well, no matter, Daniel. We all have only our day. I suppose we must be putting these things over us and make the best of what can't be helped."

"That's true for you, indeed, my good woman," said Daniel, leaning his hands on the boss of his blackthorn stick. "We're only here to-day and gone to-morrow like the birds on the bushes. May I bake a cake in your oven, if you please?"

"You may, indeed, and welcome, Daniel," said my mother, stooping down, taking some dry sods of turf from under the settle and making a fresh fire.

"I have plenty flour in that bag there," says he, getting up to find it. After a search he found a smaller bag among the other things he had stored away and putting it on the table, "There it is now," he added, "and a nice grain of flour it is too, may God increase the stores of the good people that gave it to me."

"Amen for ever," said my mother, moving towards the table, opening the little bag and emptying it into a dish where she mixed it with bread-soda and a little salt. She poured some buttermilk in with it and kneaded it into a cake. When that was done she hung the pot-oven over the fire and placed the cover against the glowing coals to heat. After five or six minutes she took off the oven and wiped the inside with a clean cloth. Sprinkling a little dry flour on the bottom she put in the cake, pressed it evenly around with her fists, got a knife and cut the dough right across into quarters. Taking up the cover she wiped it with her apron and, placing it closely on top of the oven which she hung over the fire again, she covered it with glowing cinders so that the cake might have heat from above and below.

When the cinders had burned away to ashes in about three-quarters of an hour she took down the oven. The cake was baked. She lifted the lid with the tongs and the lovely smell of fresh bread filled our nostrils. Turning the oven sideways she took out the cake and put it standing beside the wall on the table to cool. I could see the mark of the cross upon it where she had cut it into quarters. Daniel insisted that it should be broken at once and some of it given to us because he said he was young once himself and knew how nice a piece of fresh bread tasted. When each of us had got our share we thought it tasted and smelt nicer than any bread my mother had ever made. We always thought the same about any bread the neighbours gave us when we called to see them in spite of the fact that they all gave my mother credit for being the best baker in the place.

When Daniel had his tea taken he folded up what remained of the cake in a clean cloth kept for the purpose. Putting his little flour bag around this again he put the lot into the bigger bag on the floor. Then he sat down again and told my mother the news he had gathered on his travels the same as Dannie O'Driscoll had done.

When he rose to go my mother said: "Wait a minute, Daniel. There's an old hat above in the loft that belonged to the old man, God rest him. You may as well have it before the moths get at it. We have kept it covered up this many a long year but it must go in the end like everything else in this world."

Going up the step-ladder she brought down my grandfather's black bowler hat and brushed it all over. She handed it to Daniel. He examined it well, turning it this way and that until he had made up his mind about it, for he happened to be wearing one just like it at the time though brown and weather-beaten. "May the Lord have mercy on his soul," he said at last, "and on all the souls that left the house," and putting it on top of the one he was wearing he pressed it down until the brims of both hats met. Then shouldering his bag he took up his stick and, saying goodbye to us all, went wandering on his way.

There is a belief among our people that if no relative of a dead person is willing to wear the clothes he leaves after him they should be given to some poor person in charity. Where certain relatives neglected to do this it was said that the spirit of the dead person could not rest properly and would sometimes be seen wandering about half naked from the other world in the darkness of the night, shivering from the cold and missing the very garments left hanging carelessly about the house where he had died!

Besides Dannie O'Driscoll and Daniel Courtney there were many others; respectable people who never did any wrong to those who gave them shelter. Many of them suffered from bad nerves. On that account they could not agree with their own people who could not understand the sorrows of their failing and as a result they had to take to the roads. One of them might be a brother to a parish priest and another a sister to a police inspector but that made no difference for these poor souls. One such afflicted person came our way. Her name was Betty Wiseman. Although she arrived in the middle of the heat in summer she wore about seven dresses, one over the other, and the whole lot covered with a big black hood-cloak. My mother had some doubts about letting her stay for the night because she was not one of the regulars but charity got the better of her and she consented.

I was watching Betty with all my eyes as she conversed with my mother in the usual way of all the women, because her peculiar antics showed me that she was not normal. After she had taken a meal she sat down near the fire and began to search for something in the countless pockets of her many gowns. At last she drew out a dirty-looking clay pipe with a long stem and prepared it for smoking. When it was ready she put the bowl right into the glowing cinders and left it there until the clay grew red when she took it out again, waited till the stem had cooled a little and then smoked with great relish.

"What are you after boiling it for?" my brother Murty asked her.

"Sure you don't expect me to smoke it raw!" she answered with a laugh.

When she was preparing to go in the morning after having

slept all night on the settle I watched her putting on her heavy robes. She did not seem to know that I was present or else she regarded me of little consequence as so many others had done before her, for she began to sing as she rolled up the bedclothes. I was taken off my feet with surprise when I found that she was composing the song as well as singing it! I could not mistake this when she came to the words:

"Bad luck to you, Mac O'Shannissey,
You smashed my bones against the wall!"

She was referring to my mother who had done her best to make her comfortable but poor Betty's sense of gratitude was rather shallow like that of so many others. I thought of Pad Bwee on the top of Eskwee and he cursing away at the end of a spree. I ran out of the house as quick as my legs could carry me in case she mistook me for a chair and suddenly sat on me with that mighty load of clothes on her and had me smothered to death before she knew what I was. Once outside I relieved my feelings by a hearty laugh in which my mother joined when I told her the cause, and that was the last I saw of Betty in our house.

Many types of people passed through our valley in this way and strange stories were told of some of them. When my father was young, he said, an old man called Mickey the Sores used to stay in the house before the big fair of Kenmare in the month of August. Before going to bed Mickey placed a shilling against his shin-bone and kept it there all night by means of a very tight bandage. When he got up in the morning his leg was a sight to see, all swelled up, red and sore-looking. He winked when he saw my father looking at it for it was only a trick to gain sympathy at the fair. So off he went into the town and placed himself in a corner of the street where he knew most of the people would pass. There he groaned as he exposed the awful-looking shin-bone and begged for pity from the people. It was then the shillings and pennies would fall like rain into his hat as a little help for "the poor man with the sore leg." My father alone would know the secret but Mickey would give him "silence money" when he came round the corner to look at him during the day.

There was one type of travelling people that nobody liked. They were called "Tramps." They were able-bodied men who did not want to work and liked to get their food for nothing instead. They were very impudent with that again, moreover if they found women alone in the houses. Then they got what they wanted by threats. If the women were quick enough, however, and saw them coming, they would bolt the doors and keep them out. But in spite of the people's dislike they kept on coming, for they always got shelter at night in the houses where there were a few strong men in the family. There they would have to conduct themselves properly and pass for semi-decent men. At first they came around one by one but later they formed themselves into gangs and became a terror to all the countryside, going so far sometimes as threatening the police in the very barrack itself.

XIII

The Wake

IT was a bleak evening in March when I came into the house
and found the first great sorrow of my life. All my previous
troubles were only trifles compared with this.

My grandmother had been ailing for about a year now and
on the previous evening my father had gone for the priest who
had anointed her with the holy oils.

As I stepped inside the door I saw Kate O'Mahoney, Maura
Nee Lhaera and my mother hurrying about the house with
their voices hushed. She is dead surely, I thought, when I saw
the brown habit lying on a chair near the fire. My grandmother's own prophecy, that she should die in March, is come
true after all, said I to myself, my heart full of sorrow and
excitement.

When I went into the room, my mother was sprinkling her
with holy water and Kate O'Mahoney was putting a lighted
candle into her dying hand. I knelt down beside my father,
joining all those who were praying around the bed. Everything
was silent now only the sound of the low sad voices saying the
Litany for the Dying.

Suddenly Kate O'Mahoney got up from her knees and
bending over the bed she closed my grandmother's eyes and
mouth, keeping them shut until she thought they would stay
in a set position. Now and again I thought with terror of my
own death when the old women would be all around me,
shutting my eyes and mouth, and one of them squeezing my
nostrils as they did to Darby O'Keefe.

As soon as it was realised that the end had come a great cry
burst out and filled the house. I was crying too fit to break my
heart, thinking that the best friend of my childhood who had
been my support in all my troubles was gone from us, never to
return.

The women were hurrying to and fro, and others had come
in to help them. Kate O'Mahoney got busy washing my grand-

mother's corpse and when all was ready she was helped by the other women to put on the habit after the clothes had been gently removed from the bed. While this was being done I watched the others at work in the kitchen. The settle was carried from the fireplace and put into position against the wall near the back door. Two sheets were sewn together by Nellie Matt who was always a great helper in case of sickness or death, and when these were ready they were hung over the settle to form a canopy which was held up by nails and ropes to the joists above. A bed was made on the settle with another sheet hanging from it to the ground. Kate O'Mahoney took the clock from its closet, blew the dust from it, pulled a hairpin from her hair and stuck it into the works to stop the movement as is the custom when death occurs in a house. The hen-coops had been removed a few days previously and put out into the back-yard.

The corpse was then brought out of the room by my father and some neighbouring men who had come to the wake. They laid it gently on the settle. When I saw it dressed in the grim brown habit I became afraid and began to think of ghosts.

From my stool in the corner I watched Kate O'Mahoney joining the dead fingers as if my grandmother had them clasped in prayer. Her rosary beads were twined about her fingers and the long brown stockings which had been put on were sewn together at the toes by Nellie Matt.

The body laid out, a box was placed at the foot of the settle and covered with a white cloth. Five blessed candles were lit in shiny brass candlesticks upon it, throwing a bright light on the corpse and all around it.

The side of the sheet forming the front of the canopy was sewed up into tucks about a foot from each end and the same in the middle so that it hung in graceful curves overhead.

A crucifix was placed on the settle beside the right shoulder of the corpse and over it was pinned to the sheet the brown cap which went with the habit. I looked all over the habit and thought of my grandmother's words of long ago when she had said: "I'll wear that hereafter." Alas, now the time had come when she could never speak again and all her sayings had come to pass.

My father measured the corpse for a coffin with the horsewhip, tying a knot on the cord where it reached the toes. Then he tackled the horse and cart and went to Gurthagreenane to buy food, drink, tobacco and snuff for the kheershucks. Pat Mulloy went with him for they say it is not right for anyone to go alone in the night for preparations for a wake.

The house was full now, for the news had spread quickly from one neighbour to another. As the mourners came in, each knelt on a clean sack on the floor in front of the settle and prayed for the repose of my grandmother's soul; then getting up, said to my mother as she shook hands and welcomed them: "I'm sorry for your trouble, Annie," my mother answering: "I know that, indeed."

My father and Pat, having returned, began to cut up the tobacco and to fill the new clay pipes they had brought with them. When this was done a pipe was handed to everyone at the wake. After lighting them the men continued to smoke but the women only touched the stems with their lips according to custom; all but Jude O'Rahilly who sat above the settle and smoked all night side by side with Barney O'Loughlin, the hardest smoker in all the parish; his wife, Nellie Matt, often cursing him for it and saying he had a shkeoin in him for tobacco.

After midnight Pat Mulloy got a prayer book, for he was the best at reading, and knelt beside the settle to say The Rosary and the Litany for the Dead. We were all on our knees. The women's faces with their serious fixed expression framed by their black shawls, their cheeks half hidden, looked terribly mournful. Their features seemed lengthened and sharpened, giving them a look of dignity and beauty.

As Pat gave out the prayers he was answered by the people. "May the Lord have mercy on the soul of Joan O'Mahoney, the deceased here present," he finished. "May her soul and all the souls of the faithful departed, through the mercy of God, rest in peace."

"Amen," said all the people throughout the house, rising from their knees and resuming their seats.

The night seemed ages long and, as it wore away, my father took drink around and a plate of snuff, offering each in turn. As they helped themselves each person said: "The Lord have mercy on her soul." My father said "Amen" and passed on to the next. The house was now filled with the smell of tobacco and drink with many people sneezing in the corners from the snuff.

The kheershucks sat on two long rows on the benches, now and then whispering together and staring at the corpse and the lighted candles at its feet. Darby O'Keefe in particular did a lot of staring. That was no wonder indeed, and small blame to him, for my grandmother was wearing the very habit he had escaped himself by so tight a shave only fifteen months before!

My mother made tea for all the people after she had laid the table with plenty shop bread, butter and jam. It all helped to break the monotony of the long night's watching.

After a good stretch of silence a man would put his lips to the ear of the man beside him and you would hear a smothered laugh. I too felt the same inclination to laugh, though my heart was heavy and my tears falling at the thought of my grandmother dead, while on top of all that I was full of fear that the ghosts of other dead people might be coming into the wake with the living.

I tried to keep my eyes from the settle but when they would return in spite of me the small waxen-like face above the brown habit did not seem to have much to do now with the grandmother I had known.

In the morning all who had been at the wake during the night went home and others came to take their places. The old women sat around the fire telling stories, nearly all about the pookies. Now and then, forgetting the dead body, they carried on the usual fursha-forsha talk they are so fond of. One of them, Mane Foley, from the parish of Kilvanagh, asked me if we had any bees. I said we had not. "If you had," she said, "you should put a piece of black mourning cloth over each hive, because if you didn't all the bees would die."

I remember how the sharp wind used to blow the canopy to and fro as the door opened to let the mourners in and out, and the fright I got when the dog rushed out suddenly from under the settle, almost taking the sheet with him in his hurry, after hearing my father call him to help with the cattle. When I heard him barking outside I thought of him as being the only living creature at the wake who did not seem to know the poignancy of death.

On the day after that our relations and friends came from far and near to attend the funeral. When some of the old women came in they went over to the body and began to kheen. I can see them now in their long black hood-cloaks and snowy high-caul caps stooping under the canopy as they cried out in a piercing wail which was taken up by all the other women in the house. They chanted words of praise, naming the virtues of my grandmother, their voices rising and falling in terribly mournful tones:

"Wisha, Joan, a lhae, you're dead to-day;
Your limbs are stiff and cold as clay;
Mu grine gu laer ee's gu dhangun thu;
Alas! you're gone where we all must go;
Ullagoan, oan oah! Ullagoan, oan oah!"

My heart was pierced. It seemed as if the kheening women were mourning for all who had ever died in the world.

"Small blame to you to cry over her," I heard Maura Nee Lhaera say to Nano Dan of Raynamona, my grandmother's first cousin who had come across the bogs to pay her last respects.

"A good right I have to cry," she answered, drying her eyes with a handkerchief, "for she was the fine grauver nochass old creature, God rest her soul, and I'm not saying that because she was one of my own."

Going outside, I saw the yellow coffin, borne on a common cart, arrive in the yard and, standing beside it, Shaun Ogue Bawn of Dhirralahun who had come over the mountains on his white horse. He reminded me of the man from the other world who had come on a white horse also to take away my grandmother's grandfather in the days of Biddy O'Mara, God's peace to all their souls.

The coffin was taken from the cart and placed on two chairs in front of the door. The cover was taken off and put standing against the wall on the left of the door as is the custom. I could see the rough unplaned inside of the coffin as they brought it into the house and placed it on two more chairs in front of the settle. The crucifix was removed with the brown cap and the sheets taken down and put behind the body. That made the house look empty and cold. I felt a strange unearthly breeze sweep round my feet as if a host of unseen visitors from the grave were swiftly passing by. A feeling of great desolation came over me. The whole world seemed void and meaningless.

Four men with the name of O'Shannissey now lifted the body and laid it in the coffin which was already lined with hay. The settle was given a turn towards the wall, to drive away from her family the disease from which my grandmother had died. It is believed in our valley that to give the settle a turn outwards is to throw the disease on the husband's family in case of a woman and on the wife's in case of a man. This was usually done when the dead person's family had a grudge against the wife or husband.

As soon as my grandmother's body was laid in the coffin another dreadful cry broke out. Now was the last time in this world we would ever look on her face. All raised their voices in a long last piercing ullagoan. Then the brown cap was pulled gently over her face and we could see it no more. This cap gave the corpse an awful strange appearance for it looked like a Crusader's helmet. Alas, it was only too true that my grandmother was now joined in the great army of the dead.

The cover of the coffin was brought in and put on. The sound of the hammer hitting the nails seemed to be striking something terrible and inevitable in my heart. Common nails were used instead of screws which would have spared us this torture. When the lid was nailed down, the four O'Shannisseys, including my father, lifted up the coffin, carried it out and placed it on the two chairs still standing in front of the door. It was left to rest there for a while at the bidding of the old women who were careful to observe the ancient customs.

At last the funeral procession began to move away. The coffin was carried on the shoulders of four young men, each pair with hands joined, all the three miles from Coomlaegill to the grave-yard at Gurthagreenane, the men changing with others as each four grew tired. It was followed by a line of jaunting cars and common carts carrying the people, with Shaun Ogue Bawn of Dhirralahun and many more on saddle-horses at the back.

In and out among the rocks the dark procession wound its way. When we reached the cemetery, the heavy rusty creaking gate was opened, the coffin carried in and taken around the ruin of an old ivy-covered church, for it was feared that if the corpse was taken directly to the grave without first being taken about this old ruin another death in the family would be likely to occur as a punishment for the hurry.

The priest was at the graveyard, impatiently frowning at the show of superstition. A white cloth was draped across his shoulders. This was the material for making him a shirt. He got the same for each funeral he attended so that he must have had quite a store at the presbytery; making me think that he was a big contrast indeed to my grandmother's whiskey-loving brother who was known locally as "Brian of One Shirt!"

When the grave was dug the priest sprinkled holy water on the coffin, blessed it and hurried away. It was lowered into the grave by means of ropes and then the nails which held down the cover were pulled out. This is to prevent unnecessary delay when the dead are rising on the Day of Judgment, the Lord save us. We stood around weeping silently, listening to the mournful sound of earth and stones falling in upon the lid. The green sods which had been removed were replaced on the grave after all the earth had been carefully gathered so that none should be left lying on the grave of any other family. No two grave-diggers were of the same name. The opening and shutting of the grave is always done by volunteers who give their services free and willingly in our valley.

When the last sod was laid, the grave smoothed over and sprinkled with holy water, the spades and shovels were laid upon it in the form of a cross. We all knelt down and prayed for the repose of the soul of my grandmother and for all the dead that they might rest in peace. After that the spades and shovels were taken up and a bottle of holy water placed at the head of the grave. Then we all left the place, shut the gate in sorrow and went out into the village where my father gave drinks to the grave-diggers in Dan the Smith's public house.

As we made our way home my head was drooping along the lonely road as I pondered on the mysteries of life and death. I looked with sorrow on the many signs the horses' hooves had made upon the soft surface of the road in that last sad procession of honour for my dear old grandmother, and when we got home it took a long time before we could get over the awful feeling of emptiness which had come over our lives.

About a month after the funeral my father found a heifer of ours dead in the stall. Nobody had noticed anything wrong with her and she had only been bought at Ballyvourney a few days before.

Nellie Matt came in to talk to my mother as is the custom when a thing like that happens.

"I don't know in the world what's coming over the place," said my mother with a sigh, for she could badly afford the price of another heifer. "That's the second animal dead in twelve months now."

"Take no notice, my dear woman," said Nellie, "and be thankful that 'tis nothing worse. 'Tis all the will of God, glory be to His Holy Name. The likes of it often happens when one of the family dies. They say they take the animals with them to the other side and Joan must have her share as well as the rest of them."

XIV

The Bog

IT was now over twelve months since my grandmother died
and things were back to normal again, thank God. The
potatoes were planted, the corn was sown and the leaves
were out on the trees. When he heard the cuckoo my father
said it was time to cut the turf for the coming year so we prepared to go to the bog at the foot of Slievemore, five miles from
Coomlaegill. A dozen or so of our neighbours came to help us.
This gathering is called a "mihul." It goes from one farmer to
another until the work is done for all.

Early on Tuesday morning they came singing into the yard
with their shlauns and croppy pikes on their shoulders. Monday
is said to be an unlucky day on which to start work of any kind
or to go on a journey. My mother had been busy that day, however, baking extra bread, some for the breakfast, more to take
to the bog. She welcomed the helpers one by one as they strolled
into the kitchen, after the fashion of Pat Mulloy, all wearing
their white and grey home-made flannel wrappers. "Those
flannel-vested gentlemen, the Coomlaegill Fusiliers," was the
name a local poetess gave them as they passed her door on their
way to work each morning.

Barney O'Loughlin came first and my father asked him to
help in feeding the cattle while the breakfast was being prepared. He did the job gladly for he was very obliging and when
Pat Mulloy arrived they both went into the kitchen where nine
or ten others had already gathered.

"Eat enough now, boys," said my mother as they sat in to
the table. "There's a long day before you."

"You needn't tell them, indeed," said Barney, reaching for
a blue duck-egg. "They'll eat you out of house and home,
woman dear, before the night falls down."

"You won't go hungry yourself either, Barney," said Pat,
throwing an empty egg-shell at Malack O'Kane, Maura Nee

Lhaera's husband, who had turned his back to give a crust to the dog.

"Stop the clodding now," said Malack who was very quick-tempered. " 'Tis too early for that game yet."

As he spoke another shell from the opposite direction struck him. We all thought he was going to flare up and start a fight but for once in his life he did not. He only laughed with the others. That was the best thing to do of course, for everyone knew that the shells were only thrown for fun. He had a very violent temper. Once he developed a dislike for a man called Andy who lived at the top of Slievelea. He was a hefty fellow and Malack was afraid of him but he waited patiently for a slant at him unawares. It came when he met Andy with a bonav in his arms near Gurthagreenane village. Malack said nothing but walked quietly up to him by way of no harm, then took him with a thundering wallop across the face. Andy dropped the bonav, of course, dumbfounded by what happened. He did not know what was up with Malack who had cleared out of his sight like a March hare. He had an awful job to catch the bonaveen again not to mind running after the man that struck him. Later on, when someone asked Malack for the reason he said he did it "because he was ugly!"

"Young fellows have no manners lately," said Pat, giving me a sudden pinch in the side that nearly made me jump into the fire.

"Get out of my way, you blackguard," said my mother, pushing me aside, "and bring in a few buckets of water before you go to the bog."

I took the buckets west to O'Grady's Well and brought them back full of clear spring water. Then I sat down to my breakfast with the second batch of men who were just beginning to get busy with the food as I came in.

My father had the horse and cart already tackled and the first batch were preparing everything for the journey. They stored the shlauns, or turf-spades, into one side of the cart and the pikes into the other. Pat Mulloy had gone home to tackle his jennet and cart for carrying some of the men because they could not all be taken in ours.

When all was ready we set out, some in the carts and some walking, by turns. It was a glorious morning, a bright sun in the east and not a cloud in the sky. The dark brown heather on the hills made a pleasant contrast to the fresh green meadows and cornfields. The air was filled with the sweet sounds of singing birds. The men too were singing as they went along. Anyone would think they were going on a great holiday and not to work. I shall never forget that lovely morning as we went along the road, the fragrance from millions of wild flowers that glittered around us in all directions going in with every breath we drew.

Dansel O'Kane, Malack's only son, a very jolly young fellow, saluted everyone we met, saying something cheerful and funny to them all. Sometimes the answers he got put us into roars of laughter. We were all full of life and gaiety. The world was surely at its best and there wasn't the slightest suggestion of a shadow anywhere. The road to the bog ran along the base of an enormous valley. On every side lay pleasant meadows and green marshes where countless buttercups, mayflowers and daisies bloomed in amazing and delightful profusion. Little black Kerry cattle stood along the banks of a brown boggy stream and swung their tails about to beat off the flies that made their lives uneasy in the midst of all the loveliness.

At length we arrived at the banks of the Glashawee river which runs through the bog after flowing for a long way down the steep side of the great Slievemore mountain rising in majesty above. It is a yellow sleepy little river now with a few nervous trout flitting about like arrows here and there in its waters where the pools are fairly deep. It is very shallow at the ford where we have arrived but in winter it becomes a wide raging torrent fed by the great mountain rains. A dozen stepping-stones placed in a line across it helped us to keep our boots dry when we got out of the carts and went over it.

While my father and Pat untackled the animals and secured them with halters and ropes to the carts so that they might not wander into the dangerous bog-holes, giving them hay to be eating in the meantime, the men took up their shlauns and pikes and went off towards the piece of bog marked out for us by the owner of the land, Mickey the Bogs, who had several other tenants as well as us. The whole bog stretched away in front, east and west, like a great lake of brown moss and heather, with the sturdy roots of ancient oaks and firs sticking

122

up their sharp whitish-grey ends from the positions they have kept for thousands of years since the big trees were knocked down by storms and floods, then gradually covered over year after year by layers of wet grass and mosses which form the peat that sometimes rises twenty feet above them. Now that the peat is nearly all cut away only the stumps of the trees remain to show that this bog was once the site of a great forest.

I took off my boots and socks as I always felt lighter and better without them and had a delightful run about on the soft spongy ground. But Malack called after me to be careful not to fall into any of the great bog-holes and get drowned, for I was not acquainted with the nature of the place. I had been wearing boots constantly now for some time as the many wounds on my heels and toes had resulted in the growth of a stronger and more protective skin which made the friction of rough boots have no effect on them as it had in the past. But I still took delight in hopping about bare-footed on the fresh cool grass.

The work began in earnest now. "Skinning the bog" was the first thing to be done. My father usually did this on the day before the mihul but this year something had prevented him from doing it. So Pat Mulloy got a spade and as he pushed it under the top layer of peat his friend Dansel O'Kane lifted it up in pieces with his pike and threw it into the deep channel from which last year's turf had been removed. This layer is not much use for burning so nobody troubles to save it. When a long strip of the bog, about three feet wide, had been skinned, my father took up his shlaun, spit on his palms and said: "Let us make a start now in the name of God." He drove the shlaun into the rough sod and cut out a part which he lifted up and laid beside him on the bank. It was shaped like a brick and its sides were shining with the damp. Malack took it up with his pike and slung it about four yards to Darby O'Keefe who took it up again and slung it the same distance to Paddy Don't Care. Paddy threw it to Barney O'Loughlin and he laid it carefully on the ground beyond him. My father dug another sod and continued to dig more and more, each sod in turn being slung out like the others and laid side by side in even rows by Barney, making them look like a tiled floor.

When my father had cut away the top sods from about three

123

yards of the strip Dansel began to dig the sods underneath. As he laid them on the bank Pat Mulloy flung them to Michael O'Grady who in turn sent them on to Brendan O'Reilly who finally placed them in a layer inside of the one Barney had made.

Jamesy O'Mahoney cut out the third row of sods which were taken up and placed in the same order as the others by two more men on the bank.

When the fourth sod was dug only one man was needed on the bank to sling and lay it at the same time.

The slinging and laying of each succeeding set of sods took one man less each time because the layer of previous sods had made the slinging distance shorter.

The top sods are the hardest to cut because the fibres are tough and comparatively fresh while the bottom ones are centuries old, softened by the rotting of all that time and easy to cut as a result. Bottom sods make the best firing. They are like coal and last much longer than the top ones. On the other hand, when a hurried blaze is needed, the top sods are the best. They make a brighter fire if they are perfectly dry.

In the middle of the work an angry voice is heard, followed by a roar of laughter from the men.

"Blast your skin, you bloody cur, mind what you're doing!" cries Jamesy O'Mahoney, for Dansel O'Kane has accidentally dropped a great dripping sod from his shlaun and it lies across Jamesy's neck like a thick brown muffler.

"On my soul and conscience, Jim, I couldn't help it," says Dansel, cleaning away the smear after Jamesy has thrown off the sod.

The words have scarcely left the lips of Dansel when he gets struck on the poll himself with another soft sod which Pat Mulloy has thrown deliberately at him instead of throwing it out in the usual way. Pat keeps a churchyard look on his face while Dansel peeps up at him in suspicion. This is followed by another resounding laugh which spreads all over the bog.

"It serves you right, you damned blackguard," says Paddy Don't Care, at the same time throwing a sod at Malack who has his back turned in the act of trying to light his pipe.

Malack flares up, turns around and threatens to stab Darby O'Keefe with his pike, telling him in angry tones that if he escaped death once before he wasn't going to do so always. But before he can do anything he is held back by the others until his temper calms down.

Having had their laughs and fun to relieve the monotony the men get down to work again and soon a great stretch of the bank is covered with the brown dripping sods. The work is hard but the men are strong and do not notice it so much. My father, however, suggests a rest, so they sit down to talk and smoke. By this time I am getting very hungry, having lost my appetite at breakfast-time through excitement at the idea of going to the bog.

Michael O'Grady lifts his voice in song:

> "It was early, early all in the spring
> That my true love went for to serve the king
> When the small birds twittered from tree to tree
> And the song they sung was 'Old Ireland Free.' "

Like all his people Michael had a beautiful voice and I loved listening to him. Most of his songs told of the sorrows of Ireland, and the English were blamed for nearly all of them.

Suddenly, in the middle of a song, he gives a wild haloo and flings his cap into the air. "Here they come," he shouts, for his quick eye has just seen something moving in the distance. We all look over the bog towards the green fields of Raynamona, covered with the many bright-coloured flowers peculiar to the district. There we see Nellie MacNamara and my sister Bridget coming along the narrow bohereen with a donkey and cart borrowed from the O'Gradys for taking the dinner to the bog. We all join in the haloo which is answered by the girls.

Dansel O'Kane puts down his shlaun, jumps up on the bank and begins to dance a hornpipe while Michael sings for him:

> "Oh, the little stack of barley is the cause of my calamity;
> The want of a thrasher that makes me lament."

Others whistle the tune and start hopping about like birds, their hearts delighted with the thoughts of dinner being so near, the bog being a great place for getting up an appetite. When the dance is over they go off in a body towards the river-bank where the girls are already spreading out the food: bread, butter and jam, with big jars of boiled new milk which the neighbours always supply for a mihul like this.

"How are the girls getting on?" asks Dansel, always a great favourite with them on account of his gaiety.

"Fine out, thank you," says Nellie. "But we had an awful job with the donkey. He wouldn't lead or drive by hook or by crook when we tried to get him out of the yard, until Bridget brought out a handful of spuds and put them under his nose. He lapped them up and then he was willing to go. When we had him on the road he was all right. I suppose he expected another bribe at the end of the journey."

"He's like the rest of these fellows," said Michael O'Grady, sitting on a mossy lump of earth and reaching for a pot of jam which he began to spread on his bread. "He wants the bribe before he does anything."

"That's a grand sup of milk, God bless the cow that gave it," said Malack, putting down his mug and wiping his lips with the end of his wrapper.

"Grand out entirely," said Jamesy O'Mahoney. "But sure everything tastes good in the bog however in the world it is. I don't know why the big people go off to the seashore for the good of their health when they could come here and enjoy it better."

"Wisha, God help us," said my father, "the bog is for the poor and the sea is for the rich."

"Hand me over the 'Dobin O'Gilvie' before Mikeen gets to the bottom of the crock," said Dansel. "I want a little of it on my bread before he starts the licking."

Dobin O'Gilvie was the maker's name on the jam-pot, and "licking the crock" when it was nearly empty was a great habit with the young people.

"Bridget," said my father, "pour out a mug of milk to Barney. He's eating nothing whatever is wrong with him."

"The devil carry the sign is wrong with me, indeed," said Barney, stretching out his limbs and laying back on the grass. "I have my belly full already, thanks be to God."

"You're welcome to it if you want some," said my father. "What about you, Dan?" he added, turning to Dansel who was eyeing the jar beside him.

"I'll have another mug to show that there's no ill-feeling," said Dansel, winking to me.

When dinner was over the men stayed sitting around, smoking, spitting, belching and talking.

"What will people do when the bog runs out?" asked Barney who was, in spite of his general good humour, a little inclined to worry about the future. "Every year 'tis going and going. Look at all the ricks around us now."

I looked across the great brown expanse of bog. In all directions I could see the great black ricks left over from previous years by people who had lots of help in their families for cutting turf and who would sell these ricks later on when bad weather prevented others from saving theirs. Here and there I could also see other mihuls at work, for this was the time everyone got busy in the bogs so as to have fuel enough for the coming winter. I could hear the cuckoo's voice come softly from a clump of ancient hawthorns in full blossom on the opposite bank at Raynamona. The air was full of gentle buzzing from the wings of countless bees, and beautifully-coloured butterflies were flitting about among the heather. What wonders there are in nature, even along the quiet banks of the Glashawee as it flows silently at the foot of a great and lonely mountain! I feel that I am in Theernanogue and that very soon perhaps someone will come and show me over the flowering pathways and the golden halls!

"Brian! Brian!" I hear a voice calling.

"What?" I answer with a start, annoyed at being disturbed in such a pleasant dream.

"You're going to sleep, man," said Michael O'Grady who was standing beside me.

I was, surely, and a more lovely place in which to sleep and dream could not be imagined.

" 'Tis the new milk that's playing on him," said Barney.

I wondered if it had come from a cow descended from the one that used to go into The Liss of the Golden Book on his own farm, for his wife always brought us a bucket of milk whenever we had the mihul, and I felt that I must have drank some of it.

"Glory be to God," said my father, "aren't we lucky to have the fine day."

127

"We are indeed, man," said Barney, "and now is the time people need it too. I think we're in for a spell of nice weather."

" 'Tis a good thing for the country," said Dansel. "Everything looks green and promising."

"I'd rather to see things ripe and rosy," said Barney.

"I don't know all about that," said Dansel. "There's more life and hope about when things are green and promising."

"That's true for you, indeed," said my father. "Ripeness always borders on decay."

"I'd rather have it your way any day, Dansel," said Jamesy.

"That's all well and good in itself," said Barney. "But where does it lead to?"

"It makes little difference where it leads to," said Pat Mulloy who always took things as they came and let the future look after itself. "It keeps up the spirits anyhow."

"Och, mu lhoum!" said Barney. "Leaves and flowers the whole way through but not a fruit when Autumn comes! Always promising and never giving!"

"I wouldn't say that," said Dansel. "Spring brings hope for summer that is always sure to come."

"Wisha, I suppose you're right, my dear man," said Barney, giving in. "Hope keeps up the spirit like a buoy in dismal waters and youth is full of promise like the cheerful month of May."

"That's the way they live in Theernanogue and stay for ever young," said Malack, stretching himself out and yawning.

"The thoughts of youth are long, long thoughts," come into my mind and again I feel myself dreaming of The Land of Everlasting Youth. Alas, I am there, but I do not know it. Theernanogue is all around me. A pleasant country, pleasant friends and pleasant dreams enrich my life. But I am roused again for the men are up and preparing for work. Some of them look tired while others laugh and stroll about as happy as the bleating lambs above them on the mountain.

Michael O'Grady and I help the girls to gather up the ware and pack it carefully into the boxes on the donkey-cart. I feel that a very pleasant picnic is finished. A shadow of regret creeps over me when I think of the many meals taken on the banks of this river in the past by those who are now dead and gone. But there, I must not meditate, for the men are on their way to work and I must go with them. Nellie and Bridget give me instructions about making the evening tea for which they leave provisions in one of the horse-carts together with a big kettle and a few saucepans and jam-pots for the men to drink from because they are afraid to trust leaving the cups lest they might get broken on the way home.

We are all back to work again. The wet sods continue to cover the bank as in the morning. In the distance we hear Nellie and Bridget shouting goodbye as they turn the corner above the fields of daisies on the slopes of Raynamona. The men and boys shout back as they disappear beyond the snowy-blossomed hawthorns.

Skylarks sing above us all day long, their voices rising and falling like the motions of their flight. The whole world now seems full of life as the weight of the heavy dinner wears off.

But after a while the work gets monotonous again and the men begin to play tricks as before. Instead of throwing out a sod in the usual way, Pat Mulloy slings it back to the man who slung it forward, and this man, taking up the joke, sends it slithering back to the feet of Jamesy who has dug it out. He only laughs, replaces it on the bank and says: "No more of this game, boys."

Michael O'Grady shouts across to Brian of the Black Trenches, a cranky little man, minding his cows on the other side of the river.

"Hello, Brian. How are you getting on?"

"Pass the care of me," says Brian, knowing well that he is being made fun of, "and mind your own business."

"That's part of my business."

"Mind the other parts then."

"What other parts?"

"Go along to hell, you pedlar's grandson! Go back to Coomlaegill and throw a sop of hay to your starving old cows."

A roar of laughter rings through the bog for Brian is noted for his witty sayings though he is "queer in the head," poor fellow, since he got sunstruck in his young days. Before that he had been very bright in school but ever since he had to be cared for by his relatives. My father knows all this and therefore asks the boys to let him alone. They do, so he walks away quietly, the black felt hat thrown back on his head which he lifts up and down as he looks out for the dangerous bog-holes, calling out "Purty! Purty! Come back here now!" to one of his cows.

The men had reached the end of the strip and after resting a while they divided into groups and cut out the four bottom sods, spreading most of them in the hollow from which the turf had been cut on previous years after having put all they could on the bank. By evening the whole strip was cut right down to the clay, and my father was well satisfied. A long pool of black water flowed into the hollow from which the last layer of sods had been removed.

When the cutting was finished the men began to clean their shlauns and pikes with bits of moss and withered grass. Then they moved towards the river-bank and prepared to go home. The sun was lowering in the west beyond the blue peaks and there was an odd fleecy cloud moving across the eastern sky. I could not help feeling lonely when I looked at the spot where we had such a pleasant meal and where I had such glorious dreams. A cool breeze crept along the river. The birds and bees were silent, but not so Pat Mulloy. He was waiting for the carts to be got ready while someone else tackled the jennet for him as he lilted the usual:

"Hie, dee, idle, ee; dilla, dee, idle, ee;
Dally, dil, owdle; il, idle, ee, dee."

Those engaged in no particular work were amusing themselves by wrestling or bathing their tired feet in the cool waters of the river. There was no unnecessary delay for each man had to be out early again the next day at another neighbour's mihul and so on, day after day, until each family's turf was cut, so we had to leave our pleasant surroundings and get on the road for home.

We had a delay however when we reached Gurthagreenane village because my father took the men into Peggy the Corner's public house and gave them each a pint of porter according to custom. I can see Pat Mulloy now as he sits on the settle, a pleasant smile on his fat round face, his nostrils widening as he stares in ecstasy at the frothy tumbler in his hand before swallowing his drink, wiping his mouth with the corner of his wrapper and saying with a sly twinkle in his eye: "Ah, Brian, my boy, that was better than a kick from a donkey!" Alas, poor

130

Pat was so fond of drink that Maura Nee Lhaera had him nick-named "Paddy the Tumbler!" I enjoyed my own drink of Killarney lemonade, the nicest I had ever tasted. The public house delay was not long, however, and we were soon on the high road to Coomlaegill again so as to give the men a chance of attending to things about their homes before going to bed.

XV

Gougane Barra

My schooldays were nearly over. Many of my companions had already left. I was in the Seventh Class, the highest in the school, and sometimes I found myself alone because the other boys stayed at home so often to help their fathers on the land. They only came to school now and again, in wet weather mostly, for their people thought that learning was a waste of time on dry days. My parents, however, wanted to give me the full benefit of a good schooling for I expect they knew that I would never be a success at farming and would probably have to go to America where so many generations of Irishmen had gone since the time of the Great Famine.

Coming home on the last Friday in September I found Maurice O'Grady waiting for me at the top of The Dog's Rock. He had finished going to school on the previous year and had settled down to helping his people on the land.

"Hello, Brian," he said in his usual cheerful way. "I see you're still going in for the paudies."

"I am, indeed, Maurice, and I suppose I must keep going for a whileen more. But isn't it funny now that when I'm coming to the end I'm beginning to like the very school I hated so much in the past."

"That's the way the world goes," said Maurice with a thoughtful look in his eyes. "We never know the real value of anything until we have lost it."

"That's true for you, Maurice."

"Do you think will it rain?" he asked, looking up at the clouds.

"I don't know. I'm no judge of the weather."

"Why then, a Muirra, maybe you know as much about it as the fellows that are talking. There's a smuiggerla west here, Jamesy O'Loughlin, and I own to the devil, he drives me mad sometimes telling me 'tis going to rain. 'Blast your skin, man,' says I to him, 'why don't you take an umbrella to bed if you're so much afraid of it!' As far as I'm concerned I don't give a fiddler's damn if it rains from here till Christmas as long as it keeps fine for Gougane. Are you going there next Sunday?"

"I will if the day is fine. What time in the morning are the other lads going?"

"Eight o'clock, I'm told. We're all supposed to meet here at that time. If you're up early, run west and give the door a kick to wake us up about seven in case we sleep it out."

But there was no need for me to wake them for when I called to the door on Sunday it was wide open and I saw Michael, Maurice and Nellie having their breakfast in front of a roaring fire of furzey roots, and at eight o'clock they were ready with the others at the appointed place which was above our house.

"Are they all there?" I shouted up to them.

"Every blasted one," said Maurice, shouting back, "except Moll Darby, and she's always late."

On my conscience then, said I in my own mind, we'll wait for her. She never crosses the hill without a full bag of cakes on Gougane Sunday. I concluded that she was delayed by the same business as our Bridget and Eileen combing their hair this way and that to suit either the arches of their eyebrows or the angles of their crazy-looking hats.

When she arrived at last, my sisters came out of the house like two peacocks in the glory of all their fineries, and we all set off together. There was great joy in our hearts, crossing the fords of Slievelea, meeting our cousins, the O'Falveys, whose parents used to call to our house during the great floods, and facing the foot of Cunnocknahiska where we were joined by another crowd of boys and girls from the far side of the valley. Gay shouts had been passing between us since we caught sight of them. We could hear the echo of their voices in the deep brown heathery glen. We climbed the steep side of the mountain, keeping together, laughing and singing till we reached the top when we hadn't the breath for either. At the end of the turf-drawers' bohereen we sat down to take off our boots and socks before going into the marshy places at the top of Cunnocknahiska and the other mountains across which our path lay. Below we could see the whole stretch of the Coomlae-gill valley when we looked back, all its features standing out clearly in the bright rays of the morning sun. Towering above us to the west were the mighty crags of Cunnockdhoonbwee, its rugged nose looking like that of a great fairy monster.

Tying the laces of our boots together, we flung them over our shoulders and, the boys carrying the girls' as well as their own, we continued on our joyful journey. I lingered behind with Moll Darby, thinking of the sweet cakes she had in the bag which I helped to carry with her boots.

I had folded up my trousers to the knees and as I raced along my heart was as light as a bird's, my feet drenched by the water oozing through the moss giving me a feeling of great freshness.

Away to the south I could see Bantry Bay like a sheet of silver between the dark mountains. I knew it was part of the great Atlantic away to the west.

"Roll on, thou dark and deep blue ocean, roll," I repeated to myself, for my heart was full of poetry on that glorious morning.

Whenever we came to a piece of flat rock, a few boys and girls seized hold of each other and took a few turns of dance. They sang and lilted at the same time, and then

> "The tender sounds of song and merry dancing
> Stole softly over Bantry Bay."

"Come here a whileen," said Moll, interrupting my thoughts. "Give me that bageen you're carrying. I want to get a message out of it." She dipped her hand into it and, "Be eating now," she added, giving me two cakes which you may be sure I enjoyed, for the mountain air is great for giving a fellow an appetite.

We were nearing the "sprigs," a line of grey pointed stones which serve as guides when the fog rolls over the mountains. They were put there by pilgrims in olden times and still stand there as monuments to their kindness. They reminded me of the story I had heard of three women on their way to pay a round at Gougane when a black fog overtook them on the top of Filenamon, a great mountain behind Cunnockdhoonbwee. They fell over the steep side which droops to a lake at the foot

134

and all three were killed. The words of an old Irish song about them came into my head:

"Coomrue of the snow and the top of the high cliffs,
And wicked cruel Filenamon that killed the women sore."

At the end of the sprigs we reached Eskwee where Pad Bwee sat on the bauncheen long ago to compose the poem cursing the thief who had stolen his fife. After that we began to descend into the deep valley of Coomrue. I was at home among the mountains and valleys all my life, yet, looking down the awful deep descent of Eskwee to the valley below, I could not keep my nerves from trembling. We had to watch our steps; if we missed one we were gone for ever. There was no talking now or no singing but each one with all his mind watching where to place his foot. Close in front of us were the opposite mountains, dark and threatening, even in the sunshine. Across them too pilgrims were pouring. They shouted when they saw us but we did not dare to raise our eyes, for this valley is like an immense pit and we were afraid of falling into it.

When we reached the bottom we crossed the Lee—here a narrow boggy little river. We were now in County Cork. We all sat down to rest after that terrible descent. Fine pieces of sweet-tasting apple-cake were handed round and everything we ate seemed full of delicious fragrance after our long journey and the fresh mountain air.

"Will we be in time for Mass?" I asked Patcheen Mike Dan, home from America, for he was looking at a fine handsome watch.

"I guess so, Brian," said he, showing a gold tooth as he spoke, a little through his nose, I thought, and combing back his hair to look spick and span, for he expected to meet many of his old friends this day that he had not seen for years since he left the old valley to go across the ocean to earn his living.

Putting on our boots we walked along the shore of the lake until we came to the lonely island of Saint Finbar. There is a little causeway joining it with the mainland and having given our offerings at the gate we crossed over.

A dead silence now fell upon us all for we felt we were on holy ground on which the saints of God had walked. There was a strange air of quietness over all the lovely island. Though it

135

was crowded with pilgrims, you could hear no laugh, no word spoken. I felt happy and uplifted. Here was peace. Here was happiness. Everywhere the people were moving to and fro, praying, with their rosary beads in their hands. A thrill of religious fervour ran through my blood.

"Faith of our fathers, holy faith," I whispered under my breath, "we will be true to thee till death."

With my cap in my hand I walked up the stone steps into the ancient monastery of Saint Finbar. In front of me lay the grey stone walls over which the ivy was creeping and, built into them, the nine arched cells in which the holy monks had prayed and slept. I knelt on the little flagstone in front of the first cell and prayed. There were many others praying beside me. I went to each cell in turn, praying before each and, when I had finished the nine, I knelt before the cross which stands on a terraced platform in the middle of the enclosure. A tablet at the foot of this cross stated that "Here stood in the sixth century the cell of Saint Finbar."

Coming out, I prayed again among the ruins of the little chapel which lies close to the shore. Here I left a pin on a flagstone under a tree, it being the custom for pilgrims to leave some token—a match, a piece of cloth or a copper coin; in memory, I expect, of the ancient custom of leaving gifts for the monks when they lived there.

My prayers were disturbed now and again by a loud voice on the mainland. Someone kept shouting: "Ahaa, the blind! Ahaa, the blind!" When I had finished my round, Maurice O'Grady and I left the island and went towards the spot from which the voice was coming. There we found a blind man on the roadside, begging from the people on their way to the island. Each of us put a coin in his hat and his prayers to heaven for us in return were enough to send us on direct to glory in the other world should we happen to get swallowed in the waters of the lake! Several other beggars had placed themselves in prominent positions along the road, seeming to have no other object in life but praying for human beings in general. "May God Almighty bless and spare you," they chanted as the money poured upon them, "and that you may have the benefit of your round this day and for ever." I knew enough about them at the same time to feel that they were equally fervent in cursing should the occasion arise, like the woman I heard about who said "The blessing of God be after you" when a man was coming towards her and "That it may never overtake you" when he passed by and gave her nothing!

After we had watched a few of them for a while, Maurice and I returned to the island to wait for Mass. I looked around me. The lovely lonely smooth water of the lake stretched across to the grey steep rocky side of Mullagh mountain. Rhododendrons formed a border to the island, their branches bending down so that the leaves seemed to kiss the water.

The bell rang for Mass in Saint Finbar's chapel. On account of the great crowd I had to kneel outside on the grass and could not see the priest, nor could I understand what he said when he came out later on to preach in the open air, for he spoke in Gaelic, the chief language of this parish.

With the end of Mass the pilgrimage was over. I mingled with the crowd moving towards Cronin's hotel on the mainland. In front of this building hundreds of people were gathered; men, women and children, tinkers, sweet-sellers and fortune-tellers. Inside by the bar you could hardly stir a leg. It was packed with people, singing and shouting. My body was so pressed that I could hardly draw my breath, while the air was stifling with tobacco-smoke, fumes of drink and the warm breath of the closely-packed people.

When I came out into the fresh air again I saw Paddy O'Mara Moor standing under a tree in the corner of the yard, muttering to himself as usual. He nodded when he saw me for he was always friendly. No matter how early the Coomlaegill pilgrims arrived at Gougane Paddy was always there before them on a day like this. Of course this made me suspect that maybe the fairies had something to do with transporting him over the mountains in the quiet! They had some job, indeed, for he weighed about sixteen stones! It added to my suspicions when I saw his trousers still folded up to the middle of his shins, for I concluded that in his talks with the Good People he had forgotten to let the folds down, after being lifted off his feet at the end of the turf-drawers' bohereen when they found him alone on the pilgrimage and landed him safely beside the River Lee before he knew where he was. I kept staring at him from under the peak of my cap and would have gone over to

137

ask him about his wonderful voyage only I was too young to have courage enough for doing so. Anyhow, his prestige as a medium between the two worlds was too great for a boy like me to make myself cheeky enough to question him. I can see him now, standing apart from the crowd, under the lonely ash tree, making gestures with his hands and speaking with great enthusiasm to the spirits of the dead. I have no doubt but that he would have told me all I wanted to know if I could have plucked up courage enough to ask him, but I lost my chance by being a coward.

I turned away to watch the fun in front of the hotel. A little woman was handing numbered envelopes around at a penny each and shouting with a loud voice: "Come on, my hearty fellows, chance your luck and win a prize."

"Hand me here one, Mary," said I, pretending for fun that I knew her.

"God keep the light in my eyes, Brian, and is it yourself that's there?" says she, to my surprise and embarrassment.

"She must be one of the O'Driscolls from Bandon to know you so well," Maurice O'Grady whispered beside me.

"As sure as you're there, that's it," said I, remembering how often these tinkers had made their beds on our kitchen floor at home.

After paying her for the envelope I opened it and found it contained a trinket. While I was examining it the woman addressed me: "Tell me, Brian," said she, "did you see a red-haired girl about the road anywhere, her dress tipping the ground and a rag on her heel?"

"I did not then, Mary, but I'll let you know if I do."

"Wisha, may the Lord reward you for it, my decent honest boy."

"Come on," said I to Moll Darby, who was standing there enjoying the fun, "we've had enough of this," and, walking towards the island again we sat on the bank by the edge of the lake watching the water-hens swim about among the rushes.

"There's a power of people here to-day, Brian," she said. "I never saw so many in my life except at The Lake of Saint Killian at Keelmickilogue."

" 'Tis a big crowd surely," said I, handing her a bag of

sweets and seagrass I was after buying at The Standings beside the hotel.

"Oh, thank you, Brian," she said. "That's too much for you now, indeed," she added, for she always made much of the trifles others did for her and little of what she did for them.

When we had rested a while and talked about various things we went back towards the hotel where everything was in full swing as it was when we left it; fiddlers and fifers playing lively music for dancers timing it out on the road; gunmen and three-card-trick men busy at their trades; and the people at The Standings doing a roaring business in the sale of biscuits, cakes, apples and oranges. I bought lemonade for Moll as that was the least I could do in return for all the cakes she had given me in the morning when the hunger was keen on me. Then we had tea and home-made bread in a little cottage by the side of the lake and after that we went to look for Bridget and Eileen to find out if they were ready for home. We found them in the company of two boys from the opposite side of our valley so when we had all collected together as in the morning and made sure that nobody was left behind we got ready for the journey back. We had some trouble in finding Michael O'Grady but in the long run Maurice and I saw him, fine and soft for himself, sitting in the hotel kitchen, singing "My Inchigeela Lass," with a pint of porter on one side of him and a girl from Borlin on the other. You may say that he had a fine warrant to sing, but that would never get him over Eskwee, so we coaxed him to come away with us and when we had him back to the crowd we all set out for Coomrue again. You may be sure that there was neither dancing nor singing now. We were all too tired for either and, to crown our troubles, it started to rain heavily at the foot of Eskwee. There was nothing left for us but to make the best of it. It came down in torrents when we reached the top and a thick fog surrounded us. Our only hope was in keeping together in case the weaker ones failed to keep the pace. Blinding rain swept into our eyes and there was nothing but watery greyness all about us. We were drenched to the skin. When it came to that we didn't seem to mind the wet any more for we might as well have walked up to our necks in the lake before we left Gougane. The journey seemed seven times longer now than it did in the morning so we were mighty glad at last when we arrived at the turf-drawers' bohereen and felt that the danger of getting lost was over. The rain began to stop too as we went down the last hill into Coomlaegill. The rest of the journey was easy, and that was the end of our pilgrimage to The Island of Saint Finbar.

XVI

The Station

In olden times when the English government had a price on the head of the Catholic priest he had to hide like a wild animal. He naturally took refuge with his parishioners in remote and lonely places where he managed to say Mass in secret on the mountains and in the cabins of his people instead of in the chapel. As one family could not well or safely keep him for a long time on account of poverty, the danger of betrayal and other circumstances, it became necessary for him to move from house to house; the near neighbours gathering around him wherever he went, so that it became the custom for people to keep him by turns. Now that this long period of persecution is happily over, thank God, the priest can safely say Mass in the parish chapel, but the old custom of saying it in the houses now and again still goes on in country places such as Coomlaegill where it is said twice a year, each family preparing their house in turn for the occasion.

This visit from the priest is called "The Station," and in this particular year it was held in the house of Patsy Mike, better known as "Paddy Don't Care," who lived on one of the farms making the "Picture Gallery" already mentioned, in Kill, at the top of Coomlaegill. It was the first Station I had ever attended outside of our own house. We had all been looking forward to it for some days after Father Stephen had called it out from the altar as is the custom.

At last the day came. It was a fine morning in October, a slight haze above the brown heathery hills, countless colours of beauty on the fading leaves and a healthy chill in the air.

My father and mother climbed the long tiresome hill with others and I went with them. Coming across the yard I saw that the house was newly thatched with golden-tinted straw, the walls newly whitewashed and everything clean and tidy about the place. We were welcomed at the door by "The Patsys" as the family was called and as we entered we saw our neighbours kneeling on the floor saying their prayers. We joined them at once because the house was regarded as a church for the time being. When all the neighbours had gathered in and prayed they got up from their knees and began to talk in whispers because the ceremonies which were to follow were taken very seriously as a preparation for the deaths, wakes and funerals which were so sure to follow. Too sure, alas, and too soon!

A great fire was burning on the hearth and two big kettles steaming beside it. The men were dressed in their Sunday clothes; the women in their best dresses, with black woollen shawls covering their heads.

"I'll go out and see if he's coming," said Patsy, taking a stick from the corner and shutting the door behind him as he left. The time seemed long and the silence overpowering as we kept our eyes on the one small window.

"He's here at last," said Jamesy O'Mahoney, standing beside me near the window. Sure enough, there was Father Stephen coming into the yard with Thigeen Rue, the parish clerk, and Patsy with them carrying the brown Gladstone bag containing the vestments and other things necessary for the celebration of Mass. The priest and clerk looked tired. They were after walking a long distance, having left their jaunting-car in O'Grady's yard to avoid taking it up the rough steep hilly bohereen to the house of prayer.

The priest got a hearty welcome from the people, especially from Maura Lar, Patsy's wife. When he had passed a few casual remarks about the weather and the fresh air of Coomlaegill he went up into the room and sat on a chair beside the fire which had been specially lighted for his comfort. When he had placed a silky purple strip of cloth over his shoulders and said a few short prayers he was ready to hear Confessions.

One by one the people went up to him with serious faces and downcast eyes. While they were doing so Thigeen was busy making an altar with the kitchen table resting on the seats of two chairs, one at each end, to raise it, for its legs were worn away with age. He opened the bag and, taking out a white cloth, spread it over the table. He put a shining brass crucifix on the middle and a brass candlestick on each side of it close to the wall. Maura Lar, wearing a reddish-brown dress with three rows of black braid near the bottom which swept the ground, took two blessed candles from the window-sill and handed them to him. He pressed their ends into the candlesticks and placed a framed and decorated piece of printed paper against each candlestick. I could not see whether the writing was in Latin or English and though, the dear knows, I was cheeky enough in other ways, I hadn't the courage to go over and find out. If I did, I knew that when the Station would be over, some of the jeering boys of Coomlaegill would make fun of me, calling me "Father Brian" or "The Priest O'Shannissey" in derision, as they had done to others. Thigeen took out a small bell which he put on the table also. He asked Maura for salt. She gave him some in a saucer which he placed beside a new tin gallon vessel nearly full of spring water on a chair to the right of the table. He took out the white vestments and laid them carefully on the left. When he was finished Patsy gave him a clean sack which he laid on the floor for the priest to kneel on while saying Mass.

I was shivering from fear of having to go into the room alone and tell my sins to Father Stephen with no grill between us as there is in confession boxes. They say the devil takes away our shame when we are doing wrong and gives it back when we are about to confess. I am sure he was busy that morning at the top of Coomlaegill, because I felt very cowardly when I saw the great form of the priest sitting before me at the fire. However, by the grace of God, I coaxed myself to kneel at his feet and make the Sign of the Cross, leaving the rest to chance and Father Stephen, for I expected him to ask me questions if I lost the power of expressing myself. With my eyes on his boots which were resting on a clean meal-sack I got over the usual stock-in-trade, telling him that "I cursed; I told lies; I disobeyed my parents"; but the devil played his hand by getting me to leave out the sins of sex as I had no idea of how to begin the telling. Father Stephen was as gentle as a child but nevertheless I was thankful to be getting up and going back to the kitchen though feeling that I had not made a good confession by any means.

When the last penitent was heard Thigeen struck a match and lit the candles on the altar. Father Stephen came down from the room and began to put on his robes. After he had tied a thick white cord around his waist he put some of the salt into the tin vessel and prayed over it. There was a little stick like a paint-brush on the table. He took it up, dipped it into the vessel and sprinkled the holy water on the crowd. As it fell on them they bent their knees and crossed themselves, then stood still and waited.

When all was ready Father Stephen knelt in front of the altar and the people followed his example. Mass had begun, Mass on the mountain again as in the penal days! There was dead silence as he prayed and read from a gilt-edged book on the altar, but outside I could hear Coneen Patsy having the devil's own clisheerum trying to keep the hens away from the door with an old shovel in one hand and a heather broom in the other, for, be it known to you, that on some occasions these cheeky cackling pullets would make nothing of flying up on the table without the slightest regard for either the priest or Thigeen Rue, and the world knows that a hungry bird has no religion.

When Mass was over and the people had received Holy Communion Father Stephen took off his robes. Thigeen handed him a passbook. It was the little "Doomsday-book" of the valley. It looked like the one in which my mother kept an account of eggs given to the hucksters and groceries received in return. Father Stephen opened it, coughed and called out:

"Malack O'Kane; three and sixpence."

Malack pushed his way through the crowd and paid him.

"Barney O'Loughlin; three shillings."

Barney paid.

"James O'Shannissey; two and sixpence."

My father paid.

Each farmer paid according to the number of cows he had, the dues being calculated at sixpence a cow.

All the others paid as their names were called out until it came to Pat Mulloy. When he handed over his money he was short a sixpence according to Father Stephen.

"What do you mean by this?" cried the priest, a flush of anger coming over his face at the idea of anyone having the cheek to offer him less than he had expected.

"That's what I always pay," said Pat, scratching his cheek as if puzzled about something.

"I don't care what you always pay," said Father Stephen in

a blue rage. "You're down here for two shillings, and I want my dues."

There was a peculiar whine about the word "dues" that reminded me of the suffering sound our dog made whenever he was kicked out of the kitchen for misbehaving himself.

"That must be a new book you have, Father," said Pat, "but new or old, I'm afraid you've skinned me for the last sixpence."

"You're trying to skin me, that's the way with you," said Father Stephen with a nasty snarl. "But I can live without your dirty money," and with that he swept over and threw the one-and-sixpence into the middle of the fire, putting the fright of the world on poor old Maura Nee Lhaera sitting beside it toasting the bread for his breakfast.

He frightened the rest of the people also and those who had not already paid began fumbling like the devil in their pockets to make sure they had the right sum ready when he called their names.

He was only barely back at the table, however, when Pat came up to him, as cool as you like, not with the extra sixpence, but with a twinkle of devilment in his roguish eye.

"Yerra, man, sure Cooby is lame anyhow, Father," says he, as if nothing in the wide world had happened between them, for everything the priest said went off Pat like water off a duck.

There was a muffled giggle among the people.

"Who is Cooby?" asked Father Stephen, aside to Thigeen.

"I don't know in the world, Father," said Thigeen.

"Yerra, that little coween of mine," says Pat with feigned seriousness, "that you saw inside the ditch where you left the side-car, Father."

There was a roar of laughter then in which Father Stephen reluctantly joined.

"Whether you have a lame coween or not, Patcheen," said he, "you're always ready with a lame excuse anyhow."

The people laughed at this even louder than before, for it would never do to laugh at Pat Mulloy's joke and frown at Father Stephen's.

God help us, if the priest only knew, he was lucky to get even one-and-six from poor Pat who always put the pint before the pulpit. The people were sure, however, that bad luck would follow him, for he was after running the risk of being cursed

by the priest "with bell, book and candle." I'm afraid some of
my own thoughts were slipping from the ways of justice and
wandering near that big fire with the precious little coins
among its glowing cinders. How I envied Maura Lar when I
fancied her sifting the ashes after the Station was over and
picking out the sixpences like miners do the gold!

"I'll meet you all on the Day of Judgment," said Father
Stephen, still smarting under the cool treatment Pat was after
giving him.

"You'll surely give us a drink out of our money if you do,"
said my father.

There was another laugh and, good humour being restored,
Father Stephen went back to the room for his breakfast, to the
great relief of Maura Lar who was standing in the doorway
with a plate in one hand and a knife in the other, her face as
red as her dress for fear he might leave the house in a fit of
anger without having anything to eat as he had done in other
places when he was not satisfied with the money he had got. It
would be terrible to see him go off thuramussing like a beaten
child. Her eyes were beaming now, however, as she watched
his big form move towards the table. When she saw him sitting
quietly there, attended to by Nelly MacNamara in a green
velvet dress and snow-white apron, she went smiling back to
the kitchen with the plate and, placing the toasted bread upon
it which Maura Nee Lhaera had already waiting for her, she
took it up to the table just as Nellie was pouring out his tea
from the rose-painted china pot she had brought with her from
home for the purpose and which was well known to Father
Stephen on account of having seen it at so many Stations, the
MacNamaras calling it "The Priest's Taypot" on that account.
When Maura had placed the toast before him and begged him
to help himself she returned to the kitchen fire for the eggs, to
the boiling of which my mother was attending. She lifted half
a dozen on to a deep plate and when she had taken them up to
the room I could hear her urging Father Stephen to make a
good breakfast.

"Leave west as many eggs as you can, Father," she said.
"They're all fine and fresh. I only took them out of the nests
the minute after Mass was over."

I was wondering if some of them were even more than fresh

on account of having been laid before their time as the result of Coneen's vigorous use of the broom and shovel!

"Eroo, man alive," she continued, "these brown pullets are greatly out for laying. Don't be shy now. Make yourself at home. Crack your egg, man dear. There's nothing like a fresh egg for putting mate on a fellow's plucks."

"That's true for you, Maura, indeed," said Barney O'Loughlin, sitting opposite to Father Stephen who had asked specially for his company on account of his general intelligence and jovial ways, though the girls attending did not always approve of the choice because Barney had a failing for spilling his tea on the clean tablecloth, which, like the teapot, had often to be borrowed for the occasion.

"I suppose that's why you're so fat and cheerful yourself," said Father Stephen to Maura as he began to take her advice.

"Cheerful, how are you, indeed!" said Maura with a laugh. " 'Pon my honour, Father, we'll be dead long enough, God help us, and that will be soon enough for us to wear the lonesome faces."

Thigeen Rue had already cleared away the vestments and replaced them in the bag with the crucifix and other fittings. The table was lifted off the chairs which supported it and pulled out from the wall so that the people could sit around it on all sides. Nellie Matt and Biddy O'Rairdon laid cups and saucers on it for the people. Dansel O'Kane helped to cut the home-made cakes and currant loaves. There was jam and butter galore among the other good things which included a big dish of fine blue duck-eggs of which I was very fond.

The kettles were bubbling on the hob. Nellie Matt took down two china teapots from the clevvy over the fire and wiped them with a cloth. She rinsed them carefully with boiling water and emptied them into a tin basin which was used as a slop-bowl near the fire. As she reached to the clevvy for the tea-box I could see the narrow strips of white cloth she used as garters for holding up her thick home-made woollen stockings which were coloured red by a local dye called "Lis na gluc," made from a substance which grew on the rocks. Having pulled out some cinders from the hearth she placed the pots firmly on them. Putting several spoons of tea into each she poured boiling water into them from one of the kettles until they were full.

She put the lids on while Biddy O'Rairdon brought a bucket of fresh water from the well above the house, re-filled the kettle and hung it over the fire to boil again.

The first eight people were already sitting at the table, some buttering bread, others cracking eggs, the remainder quietly waiting to be spoon-fed by the women as they were at home. My mother was content to sit on the settle eating a slice of buttered shop bread which she liked very much. The talk was low, of course, in the presence of the priest, to give him the impression that Coomlaegill was a resting-place for angels as well as any other part of Killarney! Biddy put bread on the plates of shy people, urging them to eat before the others had finished off the good things. When Nellie came with the first pot of tea and poured it out, followed by Biddy with the second, they all got to work in earnest. Tea, sugar, eggs, jam and bread began to go down the red gullets, for everyone was hungry on account of the fast before Communion.

In between the gulping a whispering talk went on.

"His reverence was a bit saucy this morning," said Malack, himself no master of a gentle tongue.

"I'm telling you he wouldn't be half so stiff," said Maura Nee Lhaera, "if he had to go out and dig potatoes for his breakfast like poor Father Daniel, God rest him, had to do in this parish before the clergy got the big notions. I saw him do it with my own two eyes and, a Muirra fain, you may say he was the sweet labourer that had the fine slochtur warrant to use a spade."

"Yerra, for goodness' sake, woman dear, those times are gone for ever," said Pat Mulloy. "Parish priests are full of taspy now for the silly people go too much out of their way to make a fuss about them."

"Shut your mouth, you damned blackguard," said Noreen Na Glanna, Maura Lar's mother, who was sitting at the end of the table nearest the fire, the frills of her white cap framing her long sharp wrinkled face above her black hood-cloak and a crucifix hanging from a set of brown rosary beads about her neck. "You should let the holy priests alone on blessed days like this, or maybe the favour of the year might leave you if you don't. I'm ninety-seven years old and I never heard such talk at a Station before."

148

"Yerra, whisht your tongue, woman," said Nellie Matt who would stand no nonsense, even from the priest himself if it went to that. "Sure what they're saying is only right. And now," she added, turning to the others, "let ye hurry up and drink that sup o' tay. The eyes are watering on the others and they standing there with hungry bellies on them craving for the blessed food."

"Wisha, that's true for you, indeed, Nellie," said Noreen, finishing off her cup of tea, shaking the crumbs from her clothes and leaving the table. "I was that way myself after walking across the valley this morning."

"Faith then, you're fine and hardy for your age," said Nellie, taking away her cup and wiping the table.

I was ready to eat the limewash off the walls myself, so when the others had finished and moved away I sat in with the next batch and waited until the ware was washed. In the meantime I enjoyed eating a piece of lovely seed-cake which I liked very much. Biddy O'Rairdon put two duck-eggs on my plate when the ware was replaced on the table and when the tea was poured out I got at the food in earnest. You may be sure that I enjoyed my meal that morning.

Thigeen Rue had his food with the first batch for he never took it with the priest. Being the parish clerk he got some extra fussing beyond the others. I saw Paddy Don't Care whispering with him near the dresser. Paddy was an understanding little man, in spite of his name, and he was good-natured also. He took a bottle of whiskey from behind a dish on the dresser and poured him out a big glass full. I watched Thigeen throw west his drink with a relish that showed itself in the swelling veins of his neck. He put the glass back on the dresser without making any noise in case his Reverence heard the jingle and kicked up holy murder about having drink in the house on such a holy day. Then he wiped the whiskey-dribbles from his chin with the heel of his fist and, straightening the concertina-shaped hat on his head to take away the look of tippling, he waited quietly near the door for Father Stephen.

I was examining the little blue flowers printed on the china cups and saucers as well as the golden rims and similar flowers on the teapots and egg-stands and wondering how they were put there in such a clever way when Father Stephen came down from the room and started talking with the people. After a little bantering, in which Paddy Don't Care and my father took a prominent part, he said goodbye to us all and went out with Thigeen. Paddy helped him to take the Gladstone bag across the stone steps leading over the moss-grown fence into the field at the far end of the yard through which a nearway could be taken to the bohereen beyond.

While the priest was present the people were careful not to be seen smoking by him though some were very anxious for a few puffs, moreover Barney O'Loughlin who had no chance at all on account of having been at the table with him. Now that he was gone, however, the pipes came out and clouds of smoke went curling up to the rafters.

When Paddy returned he went up to the loft and brought down a big basket of bottles which he had hidden there.

"Wisha, more power to your elbow, Paddy," said my father. "I knew you had them somewhere."

"It wouldn't do at all for his Reverence to see them," said Paddy.

"Ish deocha fain," said Maura Lar, "we'd have war in the cabin if he did."

"Muirra then, he was hot enough as it was," said Pat Mulloy with a steady eye on the basket.

"He was then, surely," said Maura, taking a corkscrew from a hook on the dresser and giving it to Paddy who was removing the straw cover from a bottle of whiskey. "Draw that cork, Patsy, a lhae gill," she added. "These women want a drop of punch to warm them up."

Paddy did as he was told, pouring whiskey into two or three glasses on the table. Maura added sugar and boiling water. As she stirred them up the spoon made a pleasant jingle in the glasses, reminding me of Father Stephen's bell. The lovely intoxicating smell of Jameson's whiskey filled the room. When Maura handed a steaming glass to each woman in turn, they all refused it at first, saying "Och, wisha, no. I don't care much about it," but after a little gentle persuasion they threw it back in one gulp with the same relish as Thigeen Rue; all except Nellie Matt and a few others who never tasted it anywhere. I thought it strange of the women to refuse it because I would have snapped up the glass at once myself and drank it off without any force on the part of the giver the way it was kind for me, because most of my ancestors were blue drunkards, God help us. Perhaps some of the women thought there was not enough in the glass and felt inclined to wait for the second round which might be bigger. I could not say, indeed. Women are as queer as the devil sometimes, you know.

While Maura was attending to the punch Paddy was dividing the groodles elsewhere, handing bottles of porter to the men, wine to the girls and lemonade to the boys.

The whole house now began to go gay because all the people were enjoying themselves. This was the townland holiday and they were all out to make the most of it, feeling that they might never again meet in the same place, for six years must roll by before Paddy Don't Care's turn for The Station came round again. Soon the singing and dancing began. Nellie Matt supplied "puss music" by lilting, humming and singing:

"Some say the devil's dead, the devil's dead, the devil's dead;
Some say the devil's dead and buried in Killarney:
More say he rose again, he rose again, he rose again;
More say he rose again and joined the British Army!"

Around the house the dancers tripped the merry movements of the Highland Fling, encouraged by the older people who sat watching with their glasses in their hands thinking of the past perhaps when they too had tripped it out merrily in the same way themselves.

"Dal aw the dal the dal, the dal the dal, the dal the dal;
Dal aw the dal the dal, the dally dittle dairum:
Tie oo rel al the dal, the tie oo rel al the dal;
Tie oo rel al the dal, the dally dittle dairum!"

and it went on like this until the dancers had to give up from the loss of sweat and the lilter from the lack of wind.

"More power to your windpipe, Nellie," said my father when they had finished.

"Get on the floor yourself and give us a hornpipe," said Nellie.

"Why then I'll never break your word, my decent woman," said my father, going out on the floor with her husband, Barney, for they were both noted step-dancers in their day.

Nellie started lilting again and the dancers did themselves credit on the flagstones, but what I enjoyed most of all was the curious flapping of Barney's swallow-tailed coat as he hopped about in the intricate movements of a dance called "The Blackbird."

We had a most enjoyable time and I thought it ended far too soon. But the people had to return to their homes to look after their cattle and pigs and maybe an odd child too that might be after getting into harm. When I saw them leave the house one by one a feeling of great sadness came over me and it was no wonder for we had a great day there. "Good-bye, good-bye to all of you, wherever you may be," came into my mind as I thought of the earlier days when my sisters and I used to pick the berries in the pleasant valley below. As the people left they poured blessings on the heads of Maura Lar and Paddy Don't Care. "That you may be ten times better off the next time you'll have The Station," they finished on crossing the threshold.

As each woman left Maura gave her a loaf to take with her for the members of her family who were not able to come to The Station. They also took with them a little bottle of holy water from the vessel Father Stephen had blessed for them, intending to use it later on in case of danger such as storms and sickness, and for sprinkling on members of the family going out late at night so as to keep the fairies from them.

"May God increase your store, my good Maura," said each woman as she left the house, covering the loaf with her shawl, walking gracefully away as she tidied up her long dress to save it from the gutter she would have to pass over when she had left the yard.

I can see them now as they slowly crossed the fences, each in her own direction, the men helping them over the rough places. Below us lay the broad valley with its green fields, clumps of trees here and there, furzey cunnockawns with cattle grazing peacefully among the bushes, a vast expanse of brown heathery mountains out beyond, and brilliant sunshine giving extra glory to it all.

My father and mother came carefully down the rough bohereen that led to the top of The Dog's Rock, praising the

152

cattle they saw on the way while I walked beside them like a dreaming Romeo, admiring the lovely scenery instead.

This is indeed a world of beauty, said I in my own mind as we entered the house, and for many a day afterwards I remembered the pleasant time we all had at The Station of Paddy Don't Care.

XVII

Learning to Dance

THE stalks were withered in the potato gardens and the farmers were busy digging them out while the brown and yellow leaves were falling. I had given up going to school, being now sixteen years old, and feeling fit for work, I was helping my father on the land, although I had but little interest in it. There was frost on the ground and the air was lively. I could easily have a worse job than digging spuds so I made the best of things as far as I could.

Each of us had a spade with a long handle and a wooden step for driving it into the ground. We began at nine o'clock, dug on at our ease until eleven when we sat down and rested, my father smoking his pipe while I enjoyed the scenery.

Bridget and Eileen came with two buckets to pick the potatoes, sorting the sound ones and leaving the "crichawns" or little ones behind with the decayed or broken ones to be picked up later. When the buckets were full they emptied them into a sack and when the sack was full they continued filling others until they had picked up all we had dug. These sacks are usually left in the field for a week or so and then drawn home and emptied on the kitchen loft. When that will hold no more potatoes the rest are stored in pits in the field, covered first with dry grass, then with earth, and left there until they are needed.

"Brian," said Bridget, as I held open the mouth of a sack while she emptied the bucket into it, "there's going to be a dance at O'Grady's to-night. All the lads are coming."

"How do you know?" I asked, in wild excitement at the thought of a dance, there being little else in my mind at the time but merriment and music.

"Nellie O'Grady told me this morning. She was up the hill pulling heather for a new broom to sweep the house and have everything nice and tidy for the night. She called across the buigaheen to me when I went west for a bucket of spring water, asking me to be ready and to bring you and Eileen as well."

"That will be great out," said I, being full of pleasant anticipation, for we were all learning to dance at the time.

You may be sure that I hardly felt the rest of the day passing, for it was a light heart I had at work, although I could never hope to be as good a hand at the spade as my father if I lived for a thousand years, nor as sweet a labourer as Father Daniel either! I was always awkward with every farm implement in spite of the fact that I was very willing to use them and never wanted to be idle if I could avoid it.

The sun was going down when Bridget and Eileen had picked up the last potatoes for the day, so when my father and I had secured the mouths of the sacks and placed a sod on the top of each to protect the contents from the crows, we left the field well content with our day's work, my father talking about the crops in general, more to himself than to me, for all my thoughts were on the coming dance.

Darkness came down slowly and at last the time came to go into O'Grady's where we found just a few neighbours gathered together in their old flannel wrappers and working clothes, torn and patched here and there. Everyone wore their rough unpolished hob-nailed boots that sounded like a saddle-horse across the kitchen-floor of great uneven flags. There were several boys there but only three girls—Nellie O'Grady and my two sisters.

At first we lingered aimlessly about the house, some sitting on the settle, some on the table and others on chairs beside the fire talking to old Denis O'Grady who, strangely enough, was every bit as enthusiastic as any of us about the dance although he was well over seventy years of age.

It was when our cousin Dan O'Mahoney came in that we decided on starting the dance because he had a good knowledge of the sets and could lead them off as well as being able to play fine "puss music" at the same time, for we had no musical instrument nor anyone able to play one either.

Four boys stepped out on the rough flags between which there were several holes, big and little. Each of three boys asked a girl to dance with him and as I was the fourth I had to be content with the new broom as a substitute for a female partner.

We all laughed when old Denis warned me not to step on the toes of "Miss Heather!"

"Are ye ready now?" asked Dan O'Mahoney, clearing his throat and putting his right arm around Eileen's waist as he clasped her right hand with his left in a dancing attitude.

"Yes, Dan," we said, while I held the broom firmly in my hands in readiness for any action that might be expected from Miss Heather and me.

"Dum dum, dum dum, dum dauram dum,
Dum dumil um dum, dum dauree oh;
Dilly dum, dum dum, dum dauram dum,
Dilly dumil um dum, thilum dauree oh."

began Dan with a fine strong melodious voice as he and Eileen went through the first figure of a jig set called "The Victoria." He was lilting a tune called "The Peeler and the Goat" which was very popular in Coomlaegill. Away he went about the house for what seemed a countless number of times, but the real number being regulated by Dan according to the traditional rules laid down for the set. Each couple followed in turn with the same movements and there was more joy in our hearts than if we were dancing in the palace of a king.

Old Denis cheered us when we had finished. Then we sat down to rest and discuss the different moves of the set, the mistakes we had made and so on, as if our very lives depended on the performance.

You may be sure that it was not long until we were on the floor again, hopping over the holes between the flags as if they were not there at all. Oh, how I loved these dances! The world of amusement looked so pleasant then and promised so much to come.

The dancing was followed by songs from Dan O'Mahoney, Nellie O'Grady, Maurice and a few others who had good voices. The three O'Shannisseys, being non-singers, wisely followed the rule of silence. But I went on the floor for a bout of sham step-dancing which was cheered as much as if it had been the real thing because I looked so silly in the eyes of those who wanted a good laugh at my expense. I did not know that at the time, of course, until Maurice told it to me in a friendly whisper afterwards. But for the time being we all went home in ecstasies and full of gay hopes for better nights to come.

In my spare time between work and dance I roamed about the hills as usual. The lovely light-blue haze which covered the valleys in the summer had long since disappeared but I found something like it in a condensed form and of a deeper shade on the sloes which were now ripe on the bushes around the Famine Houses and many other parts of Coomlaegill. When I touched the fruit the blue hazy substance came off on my fingers and disappeared like that of the summer.

Like Pat Mulloy, I am afraid that there was no fruit too green for me. They all seemed to promise pleasure by the sweetness of their looks. No wonder then that I picked and ate them with the same delightful relish as if they were some lovely cultivated apples from the sunny gardens of the eastern world.

When I moved from one clump of bushes to another a blackbird suddenly flew out. Like me, I expect he was there to help himself to the good things while they lasted.

"Skidder ee, weep, peep, peep, peep, pee, pee, p, p," he twittered as he slid through the air and settled on another bush at the far side of the field. These birds seemed to get more plentiful about this time. They hopped about in all directions in search of food which was then beginning to get scarce on the approach of winter. Hunger made the foxes busy too and on that account we had to be careful to bring in our hens who were fond of roosting on the big whitethorn tree which grew on the great broad earthen fence, spreading its branches over the cesspool at the bottom of the yard.

At this time the O'Gradys were beginning to come on in the world. The family were all grown up and were very good workers. Some of them had gone to America and were sending money home to help the others. Those who were left made new fields and built strong fences all over the land. Then they began to improve things around the farmyard, removing the manure-heap from the front to the back of the dwelling-house and planting flowers and rose-bushes where it had been an ugly sight for so long. It was a big event, indeed, when they built a hen-house! It was a sure sign of prosperity, we thought, because most people up to then had to keep their hens in the kitchens.

Besides being a useful covering for the hens, the new house had another interest for the young O'Gradys and ourselves. It had a very nice smooth clay floor and before the fowl took it over we used it on Sunday evenings to practise dancing. A crude place indeed for such a purpose, but I enjoyed the fun there just the same, dancing away to my heart's content with Nellie O'Grady whom I did not fear so much now as when I was going to school, while my sisters acted as partners for Maurice or any other neighbouring boy who might care to join us. We were very happy then, the Lord be praised for all His goodness, because we were living in spirit as well as in body in the lovely Land of Youth, but, mu vrone, we did not notice that time was slipping while we were dancing.

XVIII

November Eve

I REMEMBER the joy that filled my heart as I walked down the flagged stairway that led beside the low wall from the gable to the kitchen door below, for I knew there was a pleasant time before me in the little thatched house of Barney O'Loughlin which was built in line with the ridges made in the fields like many other old houses in the place because it was thought unlucky to build "across the ridges" which were always ploughed up and down the hills so that the water could flow from the trenches between them. I heard the noise of talk and laughter as I stood outside the door for a few minutes to shake the soil from my boots and to make myself look a bit tidy.

My father and sisters were already in the kitchen with many others when I went in and sat at the end of the low table beside Maurice O'Grady who was having an argument with Jamesy O'Loughlin about the best way for catching wild birds during the coming winter months. There was hardly a boy in the place who did not expect to make his fortune from the sale of rabbits and birds to the local shopkeepers. This was, of course, a big delusion, but what is it that a boy won't hope for? The idea was fostered by the sneaky advice of older boys who had had their eyes already opened, but who wished to see more get into the same pitfalls so that they might have the pleasure of laughing at the victims and throwing imaginary honours on themselves for their supposed cleverness. When the "greenies" had their baskets full of lean wild birds which cold and hunger had killed they found a slump in the market just as they reached the doors of the shops and were already counting their money after brushing past other hopefuls on the way only to get a big shock on being told by the laughing shopkeepers that they did not deal in the bones and feathers of plovers and other birds that died under such tragic circumstances.

All the others sat about in bunches, each talking about the

things which interested themselves. Barney sat on the left of the big open fireplace, smoking a dirty-looking short-stemmed clay pipe in solid comfort as he always did when he got the chance, in spite of the fact Nellie Matt was constantly trying to cut down his supplies of tobacco, because, she said, money was scarce enough without old blackguards like him blowing it into the air from their blasted old dhuedeens! There was a broad smile on his red face, however, in spite of all restrictions. He sat there with as much ease and comfort in his blue eyes twinkling under his big bushy grey eyebrows as if he had a large tobacco factory preparing "the cursed old weed" right at his own back-door!

Nellie sat at the other side of the fire knitting a grey woollen sock, her needles flashing in the firelight as she moved them to and fro among the rough home-made threads. She was a great woman for industry and was never a minute idle while there was anything to do. She always found work for every member of her family as well and, not content with that, she also tried to extend the business by handing garments to be mended or socks to be darned by the women and girls who were her social visitors on such a night as this. Our Bridget was employed on the present occasion putting a patch on the seat of a pair of old trousers belonging to Barney whilst Eileen and Nellie O'Grady were darning socks for the O'Loughlin boys—a job they did not always relish, moreover if the same socks needed washing.

"Well, Brian, my boy," said Barney, turning to me, "have you any newseen at all for me?"

"The devil carry the word then, Barney," said I, "for I didn't see a sinner since the morning. I was digging potatoes all day in The Little Field of the Two Shadows."

"That will do you more good, my gorsoon, than looking for news," said Nellie, stooping her head as she stared at me for a few seconds over the top of her glasses. She was always anxious to curtail Barney's eagerness for the sensational as he was prone to wasting time discussing details about it afterwards. But I liked him because he was one of the few people in the place who did not always talk about pigs and cattle and who knew that there were many other things in the vast and wonderful world besides animals and farmers. He always bought a news-paper too and read it carefully while his neighbours never bothered to do so and only glanced carelessly over one if it came by chance around a loaf or a parcel from the shop.

It was November Eve, always a great night for playing games and tricks as well as for telling lonesome stories about the spirits from the life beyond the grave.

"Where is the tub, Mother?" asked Andy, the second son of Barney, a fine hearty good-natured fellow, full of fun and devilment, but a great helper like his mother in the case of need.

"Outside in the crow, my boy," she said, for that is the Gaelic name for an outhouse, though it is usually applied only to the cowshed.

"Come on, Brian," said Andy to me. "We'll go out and bring it in."

"Mind yourself there on the steps," he warned as soon as we got outside the door, because the way from the kitchen to the crow was like a ford on a rocky river-bed with the danger of falling into the deep manure pit on the right-hand side.

When we reached the crow-door he opened it, went in and struck a match from which he lit a small sickly little oil-lamp made from a covered golden-syrup tin with a piece of cotton rag stuck through the valve-holder of an old bicycle-tube attached to the cover doing duty for a wick. As I moved along the "corridor" behind the cows my face struck against a spider spinning his web in the dark, for it seems that Barney's kitchen was not the only industrial centre in that locality. The little creature ran quickly over my face, giving me a start which made me reach my hand up to push him off with a curse on my tongue and a thoughtless warning that he should mind his own business, which was exactly what he was doing until I came along and disturbed him. In the dim light I could see the donkey lying peacefully beside the cows who were stretched in a long row to the right of him, chewing their cuds, grunting, coughing and belching like real human beings. Two goats were lying on the opposite side of Neddy. Looking towards the loft I could see two or three hens on their perches, opening and shutting their sleepy eyes which were gleaming in the lamp-light, then starting to pick at their somewhat ruffled feathers and replacing their heads under their wings as much as to say: "All is well, and so to bed."

Andy reached for the tub which was lying near a big turf-kishawn full of turnips with which to feed the cows on the following morning.

"Catch it there, Brian," he said, pointing to one of the handles.

I stepped carefully across the channel which drained the crow under the door-step so as to avoid putting my feet on the many deposits the cows had left on their way to the stake and, taking hold of the handle, lifted up the tub with Andy who blew out the light as we reached the door.

"Leave it down here for a minute, Brian," he said when we got outside. "I must shut the door and put on the hasp. You'd never know what cursed devil of a straying animal might come in during the night and horn every cow in the place to death."

"And the donkey and goats as well," said I, "for only the hens and spiders could escape in a case like that."

"Upon my soul then you're right there," he said, laughing, "for the thieving animal might be like the Normans that killed man, woman and child when they came to England long ago."

Andy was a great boy for history. Once he got a shining sixpence from Curney O'Shea for giving the correct day, date, month and year for the battle of Waterloo, to a supercilious inspector of schools who wanted to embarrass the master by asking questions the scholars might not be likely to know how to answer. Neither was it beyond Andy sometimes too, to spur up the master himself if he found him hesitating about giving the proper wording to his instructions. But he knew Andy too well to take offence from his antics.

We lifted the tub again when he had secured the door and, having safely crossed the danger zone in the yard, took it into the kitchen and laid it on the middle of the floor.

"Rinse it out first with a sup of water," said Nellie Matt. "You'll find plenty in the barrel outside if you go to the trouble of getting it. That will help to take the smell of the cowshare from it."

Andy got a bucket, went out, returned with the water and poured it into the tub which he washed carefully with a woollen rubber taken from a nail under the end of the table. He poured the dirty water back into the bucket and emptied it in the yard, bringing back a clean bucketful which he threw into the tub. Then, after pouring in two more bucketfuls he put the bucket down beside the wall where it made a big rattle by striking against a stack of other vessels which tumbled down on top of it.

"Now for it, boys," he shouted, ignoring his mother's voice telling him off for making so much noise.

Nellie got up from her chair, however, and laying her knitting on it, went up to the room and brought down a bag of fine rosy apples, things that were very scarce indeed on account of the small number of orchards in the district.

"Here is the biggest one first," she said, taking it out and laying the bag between her chair and the wall for safety, she took a threepenny bit from the pocket of her skirt and forced it into the apple which she then flung into the tub.

"Who's going to be first?" asked Andy, standing over the water.

"I'll have a try, by the hoakey-pokey," said Maurice O'Grady, taking off his jacket, folding back the collar of his shirt and stretching out his neck like a gander. But when he knelt down and tried to catch the floating apple with his teeth the more he went after it so much the more did it slip from him. He tried and tried again but it was no good because he could not get the apple under the power of either his lips or teeth.

"Go on there, Mauriceen," said the boys. "Grasp it now and show them what you're made of."

"Yerra, his little mouth is too small," said Dansel O'Kane with a sneer when Maurice had to admit his failure after trying seven times.

"Why then, upon my soul, your own is big enough," retorted Maurice as he wiped the cold water from his head with a towel he had taken from a nail on the side of the dresser on Nellie's instructions. "Why don't you go and have a try yourself since you're so damned clever?"

"That's just what I'm going to do," said Dansel, removing his wrapper, kneeling on the flagstone beside the tub and diving after the apple as Maurice had done.

He failed in the first attempt.

"There you are now, Danseleen, my boy," said Maurice, jeering. " 'Tisn't as easy as you thought after all."

"Hold your whisht a minute now," said Dansel. "Give me another chance at it and, by the Rod of Moses, if I don't bring

163

that apple out in my teeth the next time, my name isn't Dansel at all. What is better again, I'll put sixpence of my own into the next apple that goes into the tub if I don't get this one out."

All eyes were on him now as he shook the cold water from his hair, rubbed his palm across his foxy moustache as if pushing it out of the way and dived again. Calmly and coolly he got the apple between his lips, sucked at it until he felt he had it in a secure position, then lowered his head to the bottom, pressed his teeth firmly into the fruit and drew it out of the water in triumph.

There was a cheer from the crowd as he took it from his mouth and reached for the towel to dry his hair.

"There now for you, Mauriceen," he said. " 'Tis the staying power that does it, my boy, and that's what you haven't got any more than a sparrow."

" 'Tis the big mouth that does it, I think," said Maurice in retort, "and the bristles of a walrus moustache, without a doubt in the world."

"Go on out o' that, Mauriceen," said Dansel, who took pleasure in teasing us all when he got the chance, "you couldn't take an apple out of an empty tub with that narrow little gubeen of yours."

"I don't see how an apple could be there if the tub was empty," said Maurice who was quick at repartee.

"Win or lose, however," said Dansel with a laugh, "here's a sixpence for the next turn," and, taking the coin from his waistcoat pocket he handed it to Nellie, for he was very good-natured in spite of his faults.

Nellie took another apple from the bag and, pressing the sixpence into it, handed it to Dansel to put into the tub. Then the diving went on again with others in the competition. I tried it but lost courage after one of the bigger boys had kept my head under the water for a longer time than was good for me.

When most of the apples were gone two of the remaining ones were stuck on the ends of a wooden cross which had lighted candles at the opposite ends while the whole lot hung from a joist by means of a string. This was even harder than the diving because when the competitor thought he was sure of the apple it suddenly slipped from his mouth and, before he had time to get away, one of the lighted candles was burning the hair of his head. We had great fun watching them on account of the grimaces alone which gave us many a hearty laugh.

Other tricks were played as well and these were followed by a dance with Nellie doing the musician as she had done at The Station:

"Dal, a the dal, a the dal tee airy;
Dal, a the dal, a the dal tee airy;
Dal, a the dal, a the dal tee airy;
Dal te air, a the dow ow,"

and around the house we went in a whirl of wild excitement as we tried to keep time with the music, learn our parts and avoid the holes between the flagstones:

"Till dow ow owdle, dow ow owdle,
Dow ow owdle, dal tee airy;
Dow ow owdle, dow ow owdle,
Dal tee air, a the dow ow!"

The dance was supervised by Barney who suggested the parts and corrected us when we went wrong. "Come, come," he would say in the middle of the fun as a cheerful smile swept over his pleasant face, "let us go mad for half an hour!" and we certainly followed his advice.

When we grew tired at last we sat down and then the story-telling began. We got ourselves into comfortable positions so as to enjoy the hair-raising tales we expected from Barney and Malack O'Kane as well as from others in the house for the occasion.

"Shove up to the fire, O'Shannissey," said Barney to my father who was sitting on the lower end of the table near the door.

"Wisha, 'tisn't worth my while now," said my father. "I must be going home soon, for these two rascals, Murty and Killian, won't go to bed or do a sop or a hap'orth for their mother until I go east and threaten them with the rod."

"Eroo, God help us, a lhae, that's the way with the likes of them always, the craithurs," said Nellie. "While the cat is out the mouse will dance."

"It isn't a fit night for anyone to be out," said Maurice with a sham look of seriousness on his face as he imitated a saying of the old people.

"Ah wisha, Mauriceen grawna," said his brother Michael, " 'tis at home in bed you should be yourself long ago this night. You're there with a suck on you watching every hand's-turn a fellow will make."

"Maybe a little sleep would do more of us a share of good too," said Maurice with a familiar brotherly frown.

"Talking about being out late," said Barney, "they say this is one of the lonesomest nights in the year."

It was then we knew we were in for the stories in real earnest so I tightened my wrapper around me and settled my limbs in the most comfortable position possible on the settle beside Maurice and Andy.

"It is surely then," said Nellie as she stirred up the fire, "and 'tis Malack there that knows it better than anyone else, for that was the night he saw the woman coming into the house, the Lord between us and harm, a couple hours before his first wife died, God rest her."

"Amen, a Heirna," said Malack, making a strange sound with his mouth, "hoowick; thu," as he cleared his throat and threw a big spit into the heap of ashes in the corner under the great bundle of furzey sticks Nellie had stored up in the broad chimney to dry for the fire in the morning. Then, folding the palms of his hands over the knob of his blackthorn stick, he stooped over it and began:

"I was expecting her mother at the time and I hadn't a soul in the place to do a hand's-turn for most of the neighbours were down with the same cursed sickness as she had, God help them. I was hanging a pot of spuds over the fire to boil for the pigs. They were waste potatoes for I was rooting out a few between times whenever I could get anyone to stay inside with herself, God rest her soul and all the souls of the dead this blessed night."

"Amen gu doe, Malack," said Nellie, busy again with her knitting.

"The night was after falling and the place was as silent as the grave. I had just hung on the pot and was in the act of stooping under the settle for a few sods of turf when, the Lord between us and the powers of darkness, I heard the walk coming in the

166

yard from the little well beside the bohereen. Sha, says I to myself, she's coming now, for I thought it was my mother-in-law coming to see herself and bringing in the water before her, for I was after leaving a bucket at the well while I hunted off an old goat that was after climbing the roof to eat a few blades of late corn that was growing out of the thatch. Eroo, with that the door opened and in walked a tall woman with a thin white lonesome face and she wearing a fine black hood-cloak. She said nothing but passed me into the room before I had time to get up with the turf and I thought I felt a curious smell that sometimes comes from the habit on a dead body. I took no notice at first, thinking that maybe it was some beggar-woman that herself was kind to in the past that was going up to see her and didn't want to disturb her by talking to me, for you know what a loud voice I have when I begin..."

"We do then, surely," said his son, Dansel, winking to me.

"Well and good, why," continued Malack, "when I heard her making no sound above in the room either, I thought it strange and began to recover my senses. Up I went, a Muirra, to see what in the Name of God was the matter. King of Glory, sure when I went up there was neither trace nor tidings of her! She couldn't have gone through the little window for it was hardly big enough for a hen to do that if the bit of glass was out of the frame. I says to herself, says I: 'Nancy,' says I, 'did anyone come in here a few minutes ago?' She turned her face towards me slowly for she was very low at the time. 'Eroo, lhay gill, no,' says she. 'Not a soul in the world that I know of. What made you ask, a chree?' I was puzzled about answering but I told her that I thought some neighbour was after coming to see her. 'No one in the wide world came in here since you brought me up the tay this evening,' says she, 'but a curious thing happened to me just before you came up.' 'What was that, eroo?' says I, beginning to feel afraid at last. 'I was beginning to go off to sleep,' says she, 'when I thought I felt a sharp cold breeze sweep over my face all of a sudden, but eroo, says I to myself, 'tis the weather, I suppose, says I, for November is here at the doors. Stay here a whileen with me for I'm getting lonesome in the dark.' I was only too glad to do so and we kept talking a little now and again until her mother and brothers came in. I told them nothing, of course, for fear of upsetting the creatures, and it was the luck of goodness that they were after coming, for she died about two o'clock on the following morning, may God be good to her soul."

"Amen," said Barney, who had been listening with great attention. "Two o'clock in the morning! God help us, that's the time a lot of people die. They say the souls go out with the turning of the tide."

"Ask it after the lassie with the hood-cloak," said Nellie, looking closer at the sock with a view to turning the heel on it, reminded, no doubt, by mention of the turning tide. "Cut the top the ear off me, 'twas nothing good brought her in that night. As sure as you're there she came to take Nancy with her."

"There's no doubt in the world about that," said Malack, throwing another spit in the ashes. "When the funeral was over I told my story to her mother and brothers. 'That was my sister Joaney as sure as sure as I'm a foot high, for she thought the world of Nancy,' says the mother, says she, starting to cry, and sure small blame to her indeed. 'She was very fond of talking to her at home and she always came to see us in that same hood-cloak that you saw her wearing the night she came in. You never knew her, of course, because she was dead long years before yourself and Nancy got married.' I wasn't in the better of the fright I got for years after," added Malack, quite pleased with the impression his story had made on us all.

My father lit his pipe from a piece of folded paper which he had put into the side of the fire, said good-night to everyone, warned my sisters and me not to stay out too late, and went off home alone. I wondered greatly at his courage as I had done long ago when I found that my grandmother was not afraid to die, for I imagined the bohereen outside being lined with the spirits of old women in their hood-cloaks watching their chance to pounce on him and sweep him off to the next world!

After he had left, the story-telling went on for some time again, to the great delight of us all until Malack got fidgety all of a sudden, put his hand in his waistcoat pocket and took out a shining gold watch which his daughter had brought him as a present from America.

"In the name of the devil," said he, facing the watch towards Barney, "look at the time it is!"

"A quarter to twelve," said Barney.

"Well, I own to goodness, didn't the time fly?" said Jamesy O'Mahoney, getting up from his chair, reaching to a hole in the hob for a piece of dust-covered paper with which to light his pipe from the fire.

We were all standing now and when everyone was ready we said good-night to the O'Loughlins and left the house.

When we got outside a sight of beauty met our eyes. There was nobody to be seen from the spirit world but the sky was speckled with countless glittering stars and the ground covered with a heavy grey frost. When we reached the top of The Dog's Rock I stood for a while and looked up with great wonder in my heart. Above O'Grady's Hill I could see The Plough in sparkling glory and the Pole Star with all the constellations moving around it like the hands of a clock. Away to the south over Bantry Bay the great figure of Orion was outlined in the heavens, with bright and cheerful Sirius for ever twinkling at his mighty feet. Creation is a wonder beyond the mind of man, said I in my own mind as I went in home admiring the dark and beautiful mountains that were edging on the great expanse of jewellery above.

XIX

The Scandal

IT was a fine morning in June, a light breeze stirring the
leaves, new-mown hay scenting the air and the sound of
the river in my ears as I waited for Mass with a crowd of
people lined up on the road outside the chapel at Gurthagreenane. I was looking at the three pointed windows in the
gable of the building which stood on a green bank overlooking
the valley and at the belfry overhead which seemed to be
moving past the little white clouds floating beyond it now and
again, thinking sadly of the time long ago when I mistook it
for a tin can, of the many things that had happened to me since,
how time rolled on like a great river, and so forth, when my
thoughts were disturbed by a voice beside me:

"Brian! Brian! You're dreaming again!"

It was Maurice O'Grady.

I looked at him, smiled and said nothing.

"You won't be dreaming after Mass, I'm thinking."

"Why so? What do you mean?"

"Don't you see all the strangers here from Kenmare and
Glenflesk?"

I looked around me and sure enough there were a lot of faces
there that I had never before seen waiting for Mass in Gurthagreenane although I had seen many of them in their own
parishes now and again.

"What the devil is bringing them all around?" I asked. "Is
there a game or something on to-day?"

"Game, how are you, indeed! My pity for your pate! Is that
all you know?"

"What the blazes do you mean?" I asked, a little flushed,
remembering his comments long ago on my ignorance about
animals.

"Didn't you hear the news?" he asked in surprise.

"No. What news?"

"About Rachel O'Hara. Sure the crows above in the rookery know that by now."

My heart stopped beating for a few seconds. That beautiful girl! My God, I said in my own mind, wondering if she had died suddenly.

"Is she dead?" I asked.

"Worse than that," he said.

I was dumbfounded. What must have come over her then? What could be worse than death? Did she murder someone herself and then commit suicide, or what? I kept on wondering as I saw more and more of the strange faces arrive.

"Dreaming again," said Maurice, recalling my attention.

"No indeed; not dreaming but thinking."

"Thinking, is it, you devil, you?" he commented with a twinkle in his eye. "You hadn't anything to do with her yourself by any chance?"

"Now Mauriceen," I said impatiently, "stop beating about the bush and tell me what is wrong."

"Didn't you hear everyone talking about her for the past three or four months?"

"No; I did not."

"Well, I'm blest o' God! Yerra, man alive, sure every living soul in the place noticed her. But of course you didn't."

"I noticed her a lot more than what you think. But what was the use in that when she always looked the other way if I met her on the road?"

"You didn't know how lucky you were, indeed! But I don't mean it that way at all. I'm afraid you dream too much of what is far away and see too little of what is near."

"Maybe I do and maybe I don't," I said, getting irritated and pouting as I turned my eyes towards the windows again and saw Father Stephen passing by them on his way to the sacristy.

"She got bigger than she used to be," said Maurice.

"What's wrong with that? Can't she grow like the rest of us?"

"Well, you take the crown from all the blasted fools I ever met if you can't see the point even now."

"Wouldn't you tell me straight what you're aiming at and give up trying to keep me waiting like a dying patient at a doctor's door! Tell me in six words what is the matter with Rachel?"

"Six words!" he said. "Six words! You'll have it that way if you wait a minute."

"Oh, come on before Mass begins. I think you're dreaming now yourself."

He paused; then with a dramatic movement of his face to my ear he whispered:

"She had a baby last week!"

"What!" I cried in amazement. "A baby last week! A baby, and she not married!"

"Yes indeed then; nothing short of it, and that's why all the people from the outside parishes are coming to Mass in Gurtha-greenane to-day. It will be like Gougane Sunday for all the world as far as I can see."

"But what has that to do with it? Why should they come to-day beyond any other Sunday? We had no saint in this parish to leave relics in a golden shrine for kneeling pilgrims to remind them of their ending, nor a holy well to wash the sores that doctors cannot cure."

"That's true for you, indeed. But, dhar Muirra then, if we had no saint we had plenty sinners; and, God help us, one of them is having his name put up to-day in a sermon of con-demnation on account of his dirty doings with Rachel O'Hara."

"Who is he?" I asked.

"You'll soon find out."

The bell rang for Mass and as we went up the steps leading to the chapel I noticed many more strangers among the crowd that streamed in with us. We could hardly squeeze ourselves into our usual places on account of the flowing congregation. Finally however we got sitting on the gallery stairs and when Father Stephen came to the altar in his robes we all knelt down to pray with him.

While Mass was going on there was a lot of coughing and whispering here and there, moreover among those who had no prayer books or rosary beads, but when Father Stephen had given out Holy Communion, shut the tabernacle door, drawn the screen across it and came forward to the pulpit you could hear a pin drop.

After reading a list of religious duties for the coming week and asking the congregation to pray for the soul of an old parishioner who had died recently in Australia he put down his notes on the pulpit. As he did so the women began to push back the hair from the front of their ears and the men to settle themselves more comfortably in their seats. He coughed and the noise resounded from end to end of the beautiful chapel across which the brilliant sunshine was sending coloured beams from the stained glass windows upon the backs and shoulders of the people. There were no counter-coughs to follow as so often happens in church. He pulled a handkerchief from his sleeve, clearing his throat as he did so. He blew his nose, put the handkerchief back into his sleeve, made the Sign of the Cross, looked the people straight in the eyes, paused a little, and began:

"Well, Christians, I suppose ye all know Denny the Shanty!"

We did, of course. He was in the Seventh Class when I first went to school and he was always nice and gentle to me when many of the others were rough. During the past year I had often seen him walking the roads with Rachel and they were so wrapped up in each other that they never seemed to notice me. I could see the trouble he was in now. I was naturally shocked to hear him called out from the altar by his nickname. He got that from the little house where his people lived. He was a very nice-looking boy which was probably the reason why Rachel was attracted by him.

"And I suppose," continued Father Stephen, "you all heard of the scandal that occurred during the week. I expect you did, because bad news always travels faster than good. I visited the house of his victim and I can assure you that if the walls had ears to hear and eyes to see they'd shed soft tears at the sight of that poor girl lying there, an object of pity, her life ruined by a blackguard who is after leaving the country by all accounts and letting her bear the whole burden of his crime until the day she dies. But the Lord sees it all. He may escape the hand of man but he won't escape the Hand of God."

The sermon frightened me. What would I do if it was myself he was talking about and not Denny the Shanty? Maybe I was lucky after all that she did turn away when she saw me. How could I bear to see my people with their heads hanging and their tears falling?

I turned my eyes to where Denny's family used to sit. None of them were there to listen now but their places were taken by strangers gaping at Father Stephen with a wild look in their eyes for further details of the scandal which he continued to give them for a considerable time.

I looked across also to the spot where I had often seen and admired Rachel as she sat with her people in the happy days gone by, but there was no trace of them there because they couldn't bear to show their faces inside the chapel on such a day as this, and small blame to them, indeed.

Father Stephen picked up his notes, examined them for a few seconds, then lifted up his head and looked at the people again.

"As far as I can understand from what I have heard both inside and outside of the confessional," he said, "the whole parish is gone to the devil and we must do something about it. These cursed dances are the road to hell, I'm afraid. But, to try and recover the good name of the parish I'll ask the bishop to get the Missioners from a good preaching order to come here and try to convert you like they do the wicked pagans in the lands of darkness."

When he had left the altar and we made our way slowly towards the door I wondered why he was so much against the dances. After all there was nothing wrong with dancing as far as I could see and I felt very puzzled. I had often noticed, however, that after the dances were over in the houses at night the boys waited outside the door and grabbed the girls as they came out one by one. Then they walked away with their arms round each other. Perhaps that was why the priest objected.

When I got out into the open air I saw the young people giggling in bunches but the older people had serious faces on them because I suppose they understood the implications better. As I walked down the steps to the road, listening to the babel of voices around me discussing the sermon I could not help admiring the scene in front of me; great purple mountains bathed in sunshine, rich green woods covering their bases, meadows waving where the hay was still un-cut and everything looking as if nothing terrible or unusual had happened in the world.

On the way home I asked Maurice a lot of questions.

"Why does everyone think it a crime when a child is born like that?"

"Because it ruins a girl's life. Nobody will ever want to marry her after that because everyone will look down on her and say she was a common girl of the lanes. Neither her people or Denny's can ever again raise their heads in the parish on account of the slur that is on them and they will always have it flung in their faces if they fall out with their neighbours."

"Isn't that very unfair?"

"It is; but that's the way with the world. You don't pay for a crime. You pay for being found out. And to make matters worse, the poor child that is born will have to suffer too for being the result though not the cause of the crime."

"Well, I'm damned if that be the way with them," I said, annoyed that the critics should have no pity for the innocent.

For the rest of the way home I kept thinking of these nice-looking young people who had fallen from grace, of the strange ways of the world where so much beauty is mixed up with so much tragedy, and for weeks after the event there was nothing else talked about in the three parishes but the scandal of handsome Denny the Shanty and beautiful Rachel O'Hara.

XX

The Mission

WE had a very fine summer, thank God, and the hay was saved by the time the Missioners arrived to help us on the pathways of salvation so that most of the people were able to attend in the evenings which was the chief time for the big sermons. I remember going down the Coomlaegill road on the first Sunday evening on which the ceremonies opened, whistling gaily as I went along and never dreaming of the change that would have come over me before I got back.

From all sides of the parish people streamed into the village of Gurthagreenane and when we arrived at the chapel the standings were already put up under their canopies beside the wall on either side of the gate outside where scapulars, rosary beads, prayer books and holy pictures were sold by Jack the Hopper and his brother who always followed the Missioners about from parish to parish.

The chapel was crowded again as on the day of the scandal sermon and as my usual place on the gallery steps was taken up I had to stay standing with many others at the back of the seats instead. After I had knelt down for a few minutes to say my prayers I stood up again and looked around me at the crowd of eager faces turned towards the altar and at once I thought of Denny the Shanty and of how many were expecting his case to be re-opened again to the great delight of the scandal-mongers. I noticed a whisper here and there as well as a friendly nod from one person to another and among the strangers present were many of the local Protestants who never came near the chapel at any other time.

One of the Missioners came quietly out of the sacristy and knelt before the tabernacle. He was a rather low, broad-shouldered, red-faced man with long features and he wore the black flowing habit of the Redemptorist Order to which he belonged. After he had said his prayers he stood up and turned

176

towards us. He lifted up the big crucifix which hung from his side and made the Sign of the Cross with it, then let it drop gently back into its place. He did not go to the pulpit at all but started talking quietly from where he was.

He walked slowly to and fro as he introduced himself in an easy homely manner, telling us that he and his companion who would preach on the following evening had come amongst us for our good and that we must not therefore take offence at anything they might say as none of it would be in any way personal.

I thought he was going to be very easy-going but as he gradually went on from one subject to another he got more in earnest.

"We have come," he said, "to help you to save your souls. But only God and yourselves can do that."

His voice grew louder as he went on and his gesticulations got livelier as he warned sternly:

"Save your soul at any cost! There is only one thing you can be sure of in this world and that is that you must die! You do not know where or when or how but if you die in mortal sin you're lost for all eternity!"

"That means you!" he said, pointing a finger at me as I thought, and frightening me an awful lot, "and you!" he continued, pointing to someone else at the other side of the chapel, to my great relief. "So whatever you do or whatever you don't do, save your soul at any cost!"

I was shivering in my shoes because I had never before heard a priest talk as he did. His movements fascinated me. His arguments gripped me. He seemed alive like a glowing coal and he had the whole place electrified. Every word he said came thundering out on its own and every sentence brought a message to my soul which I became fully determined to save at any cost as he had said.

"I have heard about a great scandal happening in this parish lately," he said, and the people stirred in their seats, "but I have not come here to condemn the victims of such a misfortune, for that would be like throwing water on drowned rats. No; I have come to try and put others on the right path so that they may escape the same trouble."

He tightened the cord around his waist as he looked from side to side of the chapel.

"The others mean you!" he shouted, flinging out his arm and pointing to me again so that I began to feel uncomfortable and my conscience to wake up within me. "And you too!" he added, to the others.

He folded his hands inside the broad sleeves of his habit and walked dramatically to and fro again as he sent his messages resounding through the church so that I began to think of the robed and mitred figure of Saint Patrick shivering with fear behind me in the great stained-glass window in the centre of the gable, not to mind the way I felt myself.

"You think, perhaps," he said, with a cool and easy softness in his voice, "that if you see the priest before you die you'll go direct to heaven like a crow goes to its nest. Don't flatter yourself! You'll do no such thing, for if you make a bad Confession to the same priest you'll go to hell for ever instead!"

That frightened me worse than before because I felt that I had never made a good Confession in my life, so I listened eagerly as he went on:

"It happens very simply and it happens every day. We see an innocent little boy before us in the street and pat him under the chin. He goes to school and as he grows a little older he hears the bigger boys laughing and talking about something he knows nothing about. As the years roll on he hears more and more. Then he begins to get curious and to ask questions so that by the time he leaves school he knows a lot more than what is good for him. It is not long until he finds a girl for himself. They walk along the roads at first in broad daylight but after a while the darkness comes along and off they go to some lonely place that the devil has already prepared for them. And there," he thundered, "there, in the presence of the all-seeing God, sin is committed!"

As he paused for breath you couldn't hear a sound in the chapel. He lowered his voice as he began again.

"The boy goes to Confession a few months afterwards perhaps and says to the priest: 'I cursed; I told lies; I disobeyed my parents;' but he doesn't tell the real sin."

This added nothing to my comfort because he was only describing exactly what my own Confessions were for a good number of years.

"The boy goes off," he continued, "and after a week or two he commits the same sin again with the same girl. Then he gets tired of her and thinks she's too common on account of letting him take liberties with her so he goes off and finds another. The same thing happens all over again and so it goes on year after year until he gets married. But even then he goes on hiding his sins when he goes to Confession. He sees his children grow up one by one as he did. When they go out walking he feels that they too are acting as he did. But what harm is there in it? he asks himself. Sure 'tis human nature after all, he says, and stifles the voice of conscience. Then at last his end draws near and his people send for the priest. But not then, not even then, does he tell his secret sins! He dies after making all these bad Confessions and bad Communions. He dies, and goes to hell for all eternity! Hell!" he repeated. "Hell! Hell for all eternity!"

He had a peculiar way of saying the word "eternity" in a long drawn-out fashion so that it struck terror into my heart. It really put me thinking as I had never done before.

"When his funeral is over," continued Father Ambrose, "his people console themselves saying in their own minds: 'He's all right. He had the priest before he died.' But I tell you he is not all right. He's burning in hell and all because of bad Confessions and bad Communions which were meant to save him if he had only told his sins."

I had forgotten altogether about Denny the Shanty. I felt that I was much worse than him myself. I had never seen things in that light before. I was too proud to think I could really be any worse than others but now I knew different.

He warned us all to come to Confession during the Mission and not to hide anything. I dreaded having to do so but the fear of hell made me decide on doing so without delay.

When the sermon was over his words kept ringing in my ears and as Father Stephen came to help him with his robes for Benediction I thought of the preaching of both and in that respect our parish priest was like the ghost of a pale and sickly schoolboy compared with the majestic figure of the great Redemptorist.

When the people came out of the chapel there was no
giggling among the younger ones this time, I'm telling you.
They all took the sermon very seriously. Jack the Hopper did
a roaring trade. Nearly everyone bought a religious object as
the first token in the direction of a better and holier life. I
bought a set of rosary beads and a prayer book myself though
the dear knows the money was scarce enough with me at the
time but I was willing to make a sacrifice because I felt that a
great change had come over my whole being.

Before leaving the crowd for home I looked across the valley
to the west where the sun was setting among the golden-tinted
clouds, spreading its slanting rays over the hills and hollows.
Below me lay a broad sheet of shining water where the Gurthagreenane and Coomlaegill rivers met at the foot of a lovely
wooded hillside sticking out like a shoulder at a point directly
opposite to the chapel. Everything in nature looked so beautiful
and peaceful that I could hardly believe there was such a thing
as sin in this world or hell in the next. But as I looked at the
meeting of the waters I thought of Father Ambrose and I knew
that as sure as they flowed westwards to the great ocean so sure
was it that I had left an old way of life behind me for ever.

When I went to Confession on the following day there was a
crowd lined up at the box before me. I knew Father Ambrose
was in it because I saw his name outside it on a printed card. I
dreaded going near him but the thought of the grill between
us gave me a little comfort. I got a surprise, however, when I
found him very polite and using no harsh words at all. He
questioned me as no priest had ever done before. That made
things easy for me because all I had to do was to answer frankly.
When I admitted sexual actions in my past life he frowned and
said: "Fie! Fie! These are all mortal sins!" When he had given
me absolution I felt I was a far greater sinner than ever Denny
the Shanty had been.

The Mission went on for a fortnight and as the fame of
Father Ambrose's preaching spread about the people flocked in
from the surrounding parishes so that many of them had to be
given places inside the altar rails when they overflowed the
nave.

On the last evening all present held lighted candles in their
hands during the closing ceremony so that the church was a

sight to see and then, when it was over, we were all very sad to hear the two Missioners say good-bye to us.

From that on I was a changed person. I began to mend my ways in real earnest in so far as the grace of God permitted me. I stopped wasting precious time doing nothing but sitting around the rocks and talking gibberish like so many of my age were doing whenever they got the chance. Instead, I laid down a set of religious exercises for myself so as to keep in constant touch with God and I began reading as many good books as I could lay my hands on.

The neighbours shook their heads and said I had gone astray in mine. They whispered among themselves about my supposed failing. My own people too were troubled when they saw the change that had come over me. If I had cursed and swore, smoked and spat all over the place nobody would have noticed me. That would be normal. But turning over to the books and learning was to them an unhealthy sign. It did not improve matters either when poor good-natured Kate O'Mahoney whispered to my father about me and told him that a religious mania was the worst-known form of insanity. But as I was doing nobody any harm, being always quiet and easy-going, I became a puzzle to them all. A friend of my father's from across the valley, having heard the rumours, came to him outside the chapel on a Sunday morning and whispered quietly in his ear: "How is that son of yours getting on?" My father looked at him in surprise. He was annoyed of course and answered: "I see nothing wrong with him but as little as anyone else."

Personally I felt that my mind had improved immensely. I was learning fast and every day finding new ways for spending my time. I pitied the poor boys who were content to stay as they were and wanted no change for the better. They pitied me in return, I suppose, because the striving for learning on my part was beyond their understanding and was consequently a sure sign that I was abnormal.

Alas, the news of my unbalanced mind was spreading through the whole parish so that I became an object of conversation and ridicule far beyond what Denny the Shanty had ever been. I tried to avoid the dangers that brought him into notoriety but my quaint methods had succeeded only in getting me a worse publicity myself. I even found my sister Eileen crying over me as one that was gone, gone for ever! Why couldn't I be like everybody else? she asked. Why was I shaming them by bringing the name of our family up all over the parish? Why didn't I stay the way I was and then nobody would be talking about me? Indeed she could hardly have felt more troubled if it was my name was mentioned with Rachel O'Hara and not Denny the Shanty at all!

However, I felt that there could be no turning back in my case now. I meant to go on improving my mind in spite of the fact that so many people thought I was losing it because I felt that it would go on living for ever, and the more I learned, the more I saw how little I knew.

When the wife of my old Head Master heard about me she invited me to their house, made me welcome, told me not to mind the views of narrow-minded people, showed me over the library and lent me all the books I wanted.

A new and far better world opened up before me and if I was losing a little in one way I was gaining far more in another. Although I could never get interested in farming I worked on the land day after day because there was no other job around by which I could earn my keep. And as I worked I meditated on many things and saw the great beauty of nature more than ever before.

XXI

Over the Hills

FOR a long time I had been pestering my parents to let me visit Annaweelogue which is Gaelic for The Ford of the Seagulls. My father wanted me to stay for ever working on the land where he felt so happy and content himself. If ever I showed an interest in anything else he simply smiled and said: "May God Almighty help us. I'm afraid you'll never have any sense." But if I took up a spade a smile of pleasure would come over his face and he would have a little hope again for my sanity. The sea was in my blood. All my mother's people lived beside it and I had heard her talk a lot about it ever since I could remember. At last my parents agreed, so one morning in June, a year after the Mission, my father took Bridget and me in the common cart for about thirty miles of the journey westward. Unfortunately it rained heavily when we were too far from home to return so we kept going and got drenched all over. Then, leaving us to finish the journey on foot, my father turned the horse around and went home, getting a bad fit of sickness from sitting so long in the cart with his clothes dripping. Bridget and I reached Annaweelogue safely and changed our clothes at once. But I could not enjoy myself on this visit because wherever I went I was scrutinised by the people and as I did not come up to their standard in good looks some of them openly passed remarks to that effect in conversation with my relatives who were themselves suffering very much from the idea that without physical beauty a person was of no great importance in the world. I heard what they said. It disturbed me very much and took the good out of my visit. If they said so much before my face what would they not say behind my back? Bridget got on all right because she passed the test with flying colours, being considered one of the local beauties of Coomlaegill.

I returned from my visit greatly disappointed and got down to work again on the farm. After a time however I got sick of the eternal digging and planting which had to be repeated again, year after year, and never seemed to get people anywhere apart from keeping hunger away. To me it was downright slavery only that I did my part of it willingly so as to help my people. The grey lonesome drabbiness was getting on my nerves and I wanted a change very badly. My father could not understand this, of course, because his own thoughts were so much centred on the land, nor could he think of any alternative mode of life for me. I was a problem boy to him, no doubt, and though he knew I wanted something else besides farming he did not want to allow me to travel anywhere, for he thought everything else in the world was a waste of time outside of the land. It would be no use for me to ask his permission to go elsewhere for a change because he would look on my request as a further sign of insanity and express his disapproval in his usual prayer: "God help us and save us and leave us our senses," so I secretly decided on going off without asking him and, in spite of disappointments on my previous visit, I wanted to go to Annaweelogue again because the sea was always calling me.

I had heard some wonderful stories about members of the O'Duffy family, cousins of ours from near Kenmare, having walked all the way to visit my mother's people in the past, and some of the O'Mahoneys of Coomlaegill having walked to the Lake of Saint Killian of Keelmickilogue on the Seventh of July to "pay the rounds" on the site of his church at the foot of Knockatee where many miracles were said to have occurred in the past, as well as to visit their sister who lived near it in Aurdhaeh beside the sea. These stories put me thinking. If these people were able to do it, said I to myself, why shouldn't I? After all, they were old and I was young.

It was springtime and there was a lively healthy nip in the air. I was working away, quietly and willingly, smoothing the freshly-ploughed ridges on a fine March evening when I came to a final decision. I would start off walking that very night!

I told nobody about my intentions except my little brother Killian who was my favourite. I warned him not to say a word about it until I was gone too far to be followed and brought back, for my people always thought that I was over-fond of doing what they called "foolish things," which was correct in so far as their limited ideas went. My peculiar nature inclined me to do things of a harmless nature as a private pastime which nobody else would dream of doing for fear of being laughed at on account of being different from their neighbours.

When I had finished my day's work, taken a good meal and put a big piece of fresh bread into my pocket I went quietly up The Rock by way of no harm, knowing that Killian would tell my people where I had gone as soon as ever they got alarmed; and, being careful not to be seen by the O'Gradys or the O'Loughlins, I slipped past The Windy Verge above their houses and began my long journey.

I had forty Irish miles ahead of me, but a light heart and a quick foot kept up my courage. The moon was shining brightly and with the air cool and lively I hardly felt myself getting to the village of Gurthagreenane by the side of which I had to pass. I avoided it by taking a near-way across an old quarry and soon reached the main road to the west. When I was about a quarter of a mile beyond the village I sat on the roadside near Thigeen Rue's house to take off my boots so that I might be lighter on the feet. I had no sooner done this than along came Thigeen, my love for him, muttering away to his heart's content. I had just about time to jump inside the fence and let him pass without seeing me. He was married to Paddy O'Mara Moor's sister and whether it was the muttering he did when answering Mass or the muttering he did in private that gave me the idea, I don't know, but I had a suspicion that maybe he was after getting lessons from his big brother-in-law in the cult of the unseen. I couldn't help thinking this as his footsteps died away and my own became less audible on account of my bare feet as I returned to the road and pattered along with my boots, tied together with the laces, hanging over my shoulders and my socks firmly packed into them.

There was another man too that I feared meeting. That was big smiling Harry the Chimneys, a fellow with blue-grey eyes and red shining cheek-bones. He was always nice to me as I went in and out of Kenmare, for he was one of my father's drinking friends, and he would be sure to ask me where I was going at that unusual hour. Right enough, there he was, standing at the doorway of his house beside the road! There was nothing left for me but to stoop and hide my face as I ran past like the hammers of hell. To my great relief however he didn't seem to notice me. Perhaps he thought I was a stray donkey from the appearance I put up because the roads abounded with these animals and I was wearing the grey tweed jacket that my mother had bought for me from Murty the Mills at Ashgrove in the Valley of the Sheen. In that case I was lucky that he did not set the dog on my heels. If it was a donkey he had in mind he must have rightly concluded that it was unshod, and it was himself would be the fool if his people heard him talking to an ass!

This danger past I headed on for Kenmare which I also avoided by taking a loop road along the south side of the bay that bears its name and going on directly towards Castletown Beare. It was not long before I was passing the house of Finnawn O'Duffy where my mother was on holiday long ago when she first met my father. I knew I would be welcomed there if I went in, for they were a very generous family, but I had no time for social calls. I also thought that they might start advising me to turn back, as the journey was too long, or asking me to stay with them for the night in the meantime; so I kept away from them on that account.

On my right lay the lovely Deenish Island surrounded by the calm silvery waters of the bay and reminding me of Gougane Barra, green fields and shrubberies mixed together and a big white boat anchored in the little harbour. When I had gone a little way further on I met a group of local boys who fortunately did not know me but concluded, as I afterwards learned, that I was one of the Coffee tinkers who frequented the district. On that account they decided on letting me pass by in peace, for tinkers are no joke to meddle with sometimes and perhaps they thought I was the vanguard of a band of budgeteers! So good luck was on my side all along in so far as travelling incognito was concerned.

It was growing late now. People had cleared off the road and gone to their beds. Only an odd light flickered here and there as I strolled along with no feeling of tiredness in my limbs or thought of resting in my mind. I had a certain goal ahead of me and I was determined to reach it if God gave me the strength.

I went on and on till I reached the near-way across the side of Knockatee, a pointed mountain with vast rib-like sides, rising majestically over the Lake of Saint Killian, and I soon found myself in the lovely wooded valley of Lauragh. I remembered the rich profusion of flowering rhododendrons which had given glory to the roadside here when I travelled with my father and sister in the common cart. It was raining then and I could not much enjoy their beauty, but now, thank God, it was fine and dry even if it was dark itself, for by this time the moon had gone down behind the peaks of the great mountains.

Here however an unexpected trouble presented itself. I was afraid of losing my way for I found myself at the junction of four roads with woods around me on every side at the very bottom of the valley. One was that by which I had arrived and I recognised another as the one on which I had travelled by a different route with my father and sister. I had to choose between the other two and in doing so I picked the wrong one. I had not gone far however when I saw a great mound on my right. A liss, you devil, you! said I in my own mind, beginning to get afraid of the pookies for the first time since I left home. It was The Mound of the Golden Bushes, but I did not know it at the time. All I could see was the great heap of earth out of which were growing some tall and lonesome trees, standing there in deadly silence; all the better for me, perhaps, because if any of the branches had stirred in the wind I might have dropped with a weakness from the fright. What if the fairies came out and lifted me holus-polus off the ground as they had done to Paddy O'Mara Moor and swept me back to Coomlaegill again after all my long night's travelling! I suddenly remembered that I had not seen this mound on my first journey. That confirmed my suspicion that I was on the wrong road. Making the Sign of the Cross in great fear to guard against the Good People, I turned about and, glancing quickly over my left shoulder to make sure that they were keeping to their beds, I bolted back to the cross-roads as fast as my legs could carry me. Then, after stopping for a few minutes to regain my breath, I started out on the remaining road and naturally found it to be the right one.

I soon recognised the features of the landscape from the memory of my last trip as I left the thickest part of the wood behind me. From that on, thank God, everything went well. I swept through Collerus and Ardgroom like a March hare. The only things that frightened me in the darkness were the noises made by gurgling streams and waterfalls, the puffing and grunting of cattle in the fields nearby and the clattering of donkeys' hooves as they suddenly started to run on in front of me before I could even catch a glimpse of their grey forms in the darkness; the curbing chains attached to the feet of some of them reminding me of the stories I had heard about Lucifer himself!

I had just passed the village of Eyeries when, standing for a minute on the road to change my boots from one shoulder to another I glanced eastward and saw the first welcome burst of dawn lighting up the sky over the wild mountains. It put great cheer into my heart. I had travelled all night without stopping and now the day had come at last, the Lord be praised! That gave me fresh courage to plod along, for I had still many a weary mile in front of me.

In half an hour's time it was broad daylight. I could see clearly the beautiful white expanse of Kenmare Bay on my right with a black ship sailing eastwards on it and some small boats moored in a little harbour among the rocks almost at my feet.

When I came to the next stream of clear water I sat on the bank beside it and ate my bread. You may be sure that I enjoyed it, and when I had finished I laid myself flat on the ground and drank heartily from a little pool in the stream. Then I got up, had a good look at the new and lovely scenery around me in all directions and, feeling greatly refreshed, continued my journey.

It was Saint Patrick's Day. I offered a fervent prayer, not for rain this time, but of thanks to God for having brought me safely through the dangers of the night and for keeping it dry as well. I was wondering as I scrambled up the hill towards Allihies Mines if I could be in time for Mass in the village of Cluin at the other side. When I had gone over the top I saw the great lonely deserted-looking chimney-stacks below me at last. I looked around me again with new delight, and there, spread out before me was Ballydonegan Bay with its white foamy fringes, and Barness Gap in the mountains beyond it. Through that gap I intended to go later on to the home of my

Aunt Rachel who lived near Cahermore on the other side of the last hill before me.

My heart was full of joy when I entered the friendly village of Cluin with its white-washed houses on each side of the rough high rocky road. This was formerly a great industrial centre, for the copper mines around it were the biggest in Ireland. The people were getting up. I saw a man leading a black horse along the street. I asked him for the time. He said it was nearly eight o'clock. Then I knew that I would be in plenty time for Mass in Cahermore at eleven so I decided on going there instead of waiting for it at nine in Cluin.

By now I was beginning to get tired. That was no wonder indeed. Still, I dragged myself along until I reached Barnes Gap when my last climb was over, thank God, for the rest of the journey was mostly level with a downward slope at the end.

My joy can be imagined when at last I saw the house of my aunt with its neatly-white-washed walls standing in a green field beside the road. I was not expected there, of course, especially at that time of the morning, but that made no difference, for I got a hearty welcome from every member of the family.

It was not long until I was sitting down to a fine meal of home-made cake, butter and tea which I enjoyed to perfection. Then I had to answer the many questions they all asked me about home. They wanted me to go to bed at once, for they could see that I was as tired as a dog, but I insisted on hearing Mass first, moreover as it was Saint Patrick's Day and remembering the stern warnings of Father Ambrose about the sin of missing it through my own fault.

When I went into the chapel with my cousins I stayed near the door so as to have the benefit of the fresh air for a deadly sleep was now coming over me. As the ceremony went on my eyes shut, my head drooped several times and I was afraid I might have to leave before the end so you may be sure that I felt glad when it was over at last and I came out into the open again.

When we got back to the house I went into bed at once. My aunt had made me a nice comfortable place to lie in and I slept soundly until late that evening. Then I woke up, feeling a new man.

I stayed here with my cousins for a few days and enjoyed my

time to perfection. They were all very kind to me and took me around to see the places of interest including the Blackball Tower standing sentry on a steep cliff by the edge of Bantry Bay, having been built there by the English after a threat of invasion by the French.

When my visit was over I took the western road that led to Annaweelogue. As I tripped along I could see Crow Head in the distance and a tall spear-like rock sticking out of the water beside it. The next parish was in America for I could see the great wide expanse of the Atlantic in front of me, rippling in the breeze blowing over it. Oh, that sea! How I loved it! How it fascinated me with its enormous volume of grey silvery water! The men of Columbus cried "Land! Land!" but I cried "Water! Water!" My mind was so elevated by the splendours of creation that I scarcely felt the time going until I was right in front of Aunt Kathleen's house at The Cross of Island View on the Kenmare Bay side of the mountain. She gave me a rousing welcome, knowing my ways better than the others, because she was a more constant visitor to Coomlaegill than any of them. She hung the kettle over the fire at once and made me tea with home-made bread, but what delighted my heart most of all was the lovely rich fresh mackerel she fried for me.

She asked me a lot of questions about Coomlaegill; how this person and that was getting on; had we the potatoes planted before I left; what class was Killian in; and so forth.

Her husband, Mike of Thrawanfeerla, had a nice sharp red face but his hair was completely white although he was quite a young man. I was wondering if he had seen a ghost or something like that, but I was afraid to ask him. If he had, it didn't make him any the worse as far as I could see, for he was very jolly. He didn't seem to care much about work. On that account he didn't pester me with questions about farming and cattle. He just sat on the settle and sang for a while to his heart's content. Then he started chewing tobacco for a change. "Happy, happy Ireland," he used to sing, "a happy, happy home," and it would be always such for him, it seemed, so long as he had the song to sing and "the weed" to chew!

XXII

Kenneth O'Hara

AFTER staying for the night at Aunt Kathleen's I went up the hill to visit my Uncle Walter. He was a witty man with funny comments always on his lips. The talk came easy to him and roars of laughter followed his remarks on everything he said to his companions. I enjoyed his clever sayings though I did not like his questions about cattle and land because they only helped to show up my own terrible ignorance. His wife was also a very jolly woman, fond of music and dance, so that there was no shortage of fun in the place. She was very generous as well and always forced me to the best of well-cooked food. This was very thoughtful of her because the sea air had given me an alarming appetite.

Next day I went to visit Aunt Minnie who lived on the western side of the hill beyond Uncle Walter's. She looked like Aunt Kathleen and she also treated me very well. Her husband, Brian O'Hara, was a dark-haired hardy-looking man who seemed to be very sensible. He was clever with his hands and had built his own house. Their home overlooked a little bay betwen Dursey Island and Crow Head. From their door on a fine clear day there was a magnificent view of the lovely island with its many-coloured fields and beautiful brown and purple heathery hills. Away to the west lay the three black and dangerous rocks called The Bull, Cow and Calf, around which the Children of Lir were said to have spent three hundred years before the coming of Saint Patrick.

When I had spent a reasonable time with the O'Haras I went across the valley to where Aunt Margaret lived in a lovely white-washed house overlooking the same bay. I was made welcome here also and was lucky to find that all my relatives vied with each other as to which of them could do me the most favours. Aunt Margaret looked more like my mother than any of the others, except Rachel, who also reminded me of her. Margaret and her husband were great workers, and they needed to be so, for they had a big family to look after. The husband's name was Taidy MacFadden. While I was there he kept me well supplied with fish of different kinds for which I had a great craving.

Each night I returned to Aunt Kathleen's where Mike amused me with songs and stories. I had only one ambition now and that was to get "a lift in a boat" before I left. I had been looking forward to that for a long time. My relatives arranged the event for me when they found what was in my mind, so one evening Mike took me out on the road and introduced me to a crowd of men on their way to the harbour of Annaweelogue to haul their nets, telling them what I wanted. I went along with them very shyly but when they told me that most of them were my cousins I felt more at ease.

I am now coming to one of the pleasantest experiences of my whole life. It came to me in quite an unexpected way and brought me so many hours of happiness later on that the thought of it often brings the tears to my eyes.

Though the men and boys with whom I travelled to the harbour were my cousins some of them were inclined to make fun of me when they found that I was so shy and at the same time so very anxious to get into a boat; their own ambition being to get out of it whenever they got the chance, like me and the farming!

When we came to the little sloping pier in the harbour four of them stepped carelessly into the boat which was moored near it and asked me to follow them. They laughed when they saw how carefully I put my foot across like a woman on a slippery stepping-stone. When I sat down with them in the boat they rowed away from the pier and steered for a rocky island a little way out. When we landed there I found myself on a little beach called The Strand of Cooltraaig. Others were already there collecting stones with which to weigh down the nets after hauling. Among them was a young fellow about my own age with a big grey woollen cap falling over his eyes. I didn't take much notice of him until we entered the boat again and I was put sitting beside him so that I might help him to row with the heavy oar he held in his hands. I made excuses for being so awkward at the job, telling him that the sea and the boats were all a mystery to me on account of having lived inland all my life. "So, 'tis all a mystery to you," he said, and I noticed what a lovely soft velvety voice he had. "I'll tell you all I can about it then," and he went on to describe the wonders of the ocean in simple language for me. As we pulled out into the open sea I began to feel happy in his presence as he told me very gently how to "feather" the oar so that instead of bringing it back broadside against the wind after each stroke we were to use it in such a way that it cut through it instead.

I was all eagerness asking him about the sea, the boats and the fish. He explained everything to me in local terms and half the names he used were Gaelic. Fish, rocks and nearly everything around us had Gaelic names. Every move with the fishing in general was described in language completely new to me. I felt as if I had arrived in a foreign country. When I asked questions in the Coomlaegill way the men laughed heartily at my quaint expressions. I thought they were laughing at me personally. Half and half, I suppose.

But if the others laughed in a way that was not flattering, it was not so with the boy beside me. Instead, he seemed very eager to help me by every means in his power. His lovely soft voice was spreading a delightful charm over my whole being. I listened closely to every word he said, for it seemed as if an angel from the halls of paradise was sitting there beside me. He was treating me with such polite respect as no other boy had ever done before. I wondered why. All the boys I had ever known were, however friendly in other ways, a bit rough-spoken and rather crude in their dealings with me. This boy was entirely different. It was dark now, for the night had fallen quickly and a fog had come with it. I had not noticed the time going while this delightful boy was talking. Then suddenly, to my great surprise, I saw lights appearing in the water whenever the oars disturbed it. I never before knew that this happened but my new friend explained that it was by means of these lights on dark nights that people could see the movements of the fish below and spread their nets accordingly. They fish but little during moonlight because these lights cannot then be seen. I was all excitement as my friend kept on telling me about the sea in general on which he seemed to feel very much at home himself. I could not see his face any more, only its outline under the big cap.

When the men had hauled up their nets, taking the mackerel from them to store in the bottom of the boat, they let them down again so as to be in position for the night, buoyed up with corks and weighed down with stones. After that they rowed slowly back to the pier and moored the boat. I felt very happy now that I was after having a lift in a boat at long last for it had been one of the great ambitions of my life. I felt double happy that on the same occasion I had, without any expectation, met with such a charming companion to explain things to me.

Each man took up his share of fish and went home. I thought my friend was about to do the same but, to my great delight, he stayed with me and we walked along the road together. I was greatly charmed, because I felt that now at last I had found somebody who could understand my ways, be sympathetic towards me, and entertain me with the rich melody of a lovely voice and friendly manner.

"What is your name?" I asked, as we walked along by the Three Strands of Annaweelogue where I could hear the gentle lapping of the waves on the shingle below, for by now he had so completely enchanted me that I dreaded losing him and that I might not be able to find his likes again.

"My name, is it?" he asked in surprise. "I thought you knew it, man. I know yours for I heard you were about. My uncle Brian is married to your aunt on the side of the western hill. My name is Kenneth O'Hara."

He had already been calling me by my Christian name, having learnt it from the others beforehand. I was still under the influence of the delightful atmosphere he had spread about me when we arrived at the steps leading up to my Aunt Kathleen's door. There we prepared to part for the night after arranging to meet again on the following evening.

"Here you are, Brian," he said, handing me two fine mackerel from the ones he was carrying. "Have a fry for yourself."

"Oh, thank you very much," I said, and then we parted.

I was very glad to get these fishes which, coming from such a friend, were appreciated far more than if they had come from anyone else.

I went to bed in ecstasies and could think of nothing else but this glorious boy. My old hatred for the rough uncouth jeering lads I had known in the past was killed for ever; killed too by a complete stranger who had reversed their ignorant ways of dealing with me by using gentleness and courtesy instead of rudeness and sarcasm.

When I told my Aunt Kathleen about him and showed her the fishes he had given me she said she knew him well, adding the remark that Kenneth O'Hara was a very good-natured boy.

When I came to the appointed place on the following evening he was standing among a crowd of others and I hardly knew him because the big cap was missing as well as the yellow suit of oilskins he was wearing on the previous night. He looked quite smart as he talked and joked with the other boys. When he saw the shy and puzzled look on my face he came away from the crowd and started talking to me. There was no mistaking that voice, but it was then I got the most pleasant surprise of all when I found that his face too was lovely to look at. He had fair wavy hair, perfectly-chiselled features, blue eyes, shapely deep-red lips and a set of wonderfully beautiful white teeth which appeared as a circle of glory in his mouth when he smiled in his own magnificent way. He had a fine figure too and looked perfect in every way in my eyes.

For the first time in my life I began to forget my own ugliness. As I walked along with him I thought only of the joy that my new friend should be so very beautiful. It did not matter any more now what I looked like myself so long as this handsome young fellow thought me good enough to be his companion. Dear lovely Kenneth, you were my genuine friend and comrade surely. If I lived for a hundred million years I could never forget your sweet smiling face or the charming delightful way in which you treated me.

From now on we met on every night that he was free from fishing. He took me about with him to the houses where he and his companions went scureecthing and soon I got to know nearly everyone in the place. They all seemed to know me beforehand as is usual when a stranger comes into a country district. They were full of good nature and good humour so that it was not long before I began to love the place and didn't want to leave it at all.

My first intention was to stay for about a week but this chance meeting with Kenneth had changed all that. I consoled myself that at home my father would be able to cope with the farm work without me. After all, Murteen was a big boy now and well able to work if he wanted to do it. He was clever, though; for while I kept my nose to the grindstone, he lounged about doing nothing, nor was he asked to do it either while I was willing. Perhaps my absence would make my father urge him on a bit, for I was tired of being the drudge, while Murteen, "the good-looking, cute little fellow," that everyone admired, was having the life of a gentleman. At the end of the third week, however, a letter came from home asking me to come back as I had been cadging long enough and my people were getting ashamed of me for it. I had not thought of it that way, but then my sense of honour was touched and I prepared to return at once. It was with many regrets that I parted with Kenneth and the other new friends I had made, but I promised to return later.

My father brought the horse and cart to meet me on the return journey. He had "a puss" on him on account of my leaving home as I did and he pouted a lot. I was disappointed when I found that he did not appreciate the fact that I had greatly enjoyed the trip and that it was a relief to my strained mind to have had such a pleasant change from the drab life I had been leading on the farm at Coomlaegill. He did not know of course that I hated farming as much as he loved it and that I was just beginning to look for something better. How could he account for my ideas when the chief desire of everyone about was for land and cattle! At the same time I must admit frankly that I did not fully understand the great sorrow I had brought on the family by going off in the night and leaving them to fret in case I got lost and so forth. However, it was not long before I was back to work again and soon made up for my absence. But my thoughts kept wandering, always wandering towards the western sea and the beautiful friend I had found upon its waters.

XXIII

Fiddles and Bagpipes

EVER since I can remember I had always been mad about music. I recollect well when my sisters and I put our money together and I went over to Joseph O'Leary's near the school and bought a melodeon. On my way home it was grand to hear it cracking sweetly as I pressed the keys and worked the bellows when I got to a lonely hollow near The Pool of the Frogs.

To learn to play it we went for lessons to Shaun Heila, who was a very good musician. Many a frosty night Bridget and I ran barefoot across the wild lonely slieve that led to his house at the foot of a grey rock near the banks of the river to pick up tunes from him. The slieve was said to be a haunt of Jack o' the Lantern, and every time we crossed it we looked around us fearfully, wondering if we would see his light. But nothing would have daunted me with the joy I felt to be learning a power of tunes because it kept me occupied and helped to break the monotony.

I still went to the dances all over the valley and enjoyed them very much. There was little to fear from the girls because none of them ever bothered me on account of my being so plain-looking and having the name of being "very odd" as well. But the dear knows, when all is said and done, maybe I was a damned sight better off being spared the sleepless nights of trouble that might follow if a host of hasty females took a fancy to my face.

When I had learned a lot of tunes on the melodeon I began to long for a fiddle. But I could never get one. Fellows with fiddles would not lend me theirs because I could not play. And how on earth was I to learn to play when I had not got one? They gave me the impression that a fiddle was a very delicate machine which people like me might put out of order by merely looking sideways at it. I ground my teeth with vexation,

197

and I said to myself that, whatever the difficulties, I would some day have a fiddle for myself, with the help of God.

Then one evening, when he came home from school, my brother Killian told me that he had seen a fiddle in Joseph O'Leary's shop window.

"Is it big?" said I.

"'Tis not," said he. "'Tis only a small little fiddleen."

"Are there any strings on it?" said I.

"There are," said he.

"All right then; I'll go over to-night to see it."

When night came I ran off to Joseph's in a fever of wild excitement, hurrying for fear someone else might get it before me, for I thought everyone was as crazy for music as myself.

But I need not have worried. All was well. There it was, still in the window. I went in, bought it for a shilling, put it under my jacket and carried it home. When I got into the house I began at once to test it. I tightened the strings, rubbed resin on the bow and drew it across them. Glory be to God! Out came a tiny sweet sound! I was delighted. If I had come in for a fortune I would not have been so pleased as I was when I found that this cheap little toy fiddle had music in it. I leapt and danced over the floor for joy. Then I put my fingers on the strings, one after the other, and I nearly went mad altogether when I found myself producing real notes.

The next day as I worked in the fields I began to think over what had happened. I had looked inside of the little fiddle and found to my great surprise that it was completely empty! Not even the shadow of a wheel or a spring, and yet it made sweeter sounds than a ticking clock with all its works and trick-a-mee-jigs, when I drew a few resined hairs across it! When this happens on such a toy piece of timber in so simple a manner, said I to myself, why shouldn't it happen if I tie strings on larger things?

So when the day's work was over on the farm I got an old tin canister and nailed a piece of stick, the length of a fiddle, on it. I tied a string from the top of the tin to the bottom of the stick in such a way that I could tighten it by means of a key. Now I put a little bridge on the tin under the string which I tightened up. I drew the bow across it. Wonder of wonders!

Out came a glorious full mellow sound. Again I was fit for an asylum!

When I had recovered from my first delirious joy over my discovery, I made further experiments. Shaping the end of the stick like that of a real fiddle, I put four keys on it, to which I attached four strings. I tightened each string a little more than the one next to it. Then I drew the bow. The grandest music filled the house.

The next thing was to learn to play. I had no one to teach me, but by trying again and again, before very long I discovered a method of my own by which I taught myself, and soon I had learned a good lot of tunes. "Wisha, God bless us and save us, Brian," said the kind old neighbours, "you must be in the fairies as sure as you're there, when you can do all these things."

I now began to tie strings to every tin I could lay hands on, so that soon the house was so full of fiddles that I felt like the man in the fairy story who wished for gold and it showered down on him until he was buried alive beneath it. I gave a fiddle to everyone who had a wish for music, and every cow's tail suffered, as I had to cut off the long hairs and wash them to make the bows. Upon my soul then, there is a fine fiddler in our valley to-day who first learned to play on one of my fiddles. And now the old fiddlers who wouldn't lend me their fiddles when I had none of my own, were quite willing to do so when I had no need of them, and I thought of the old proverb: "Have it yourself or be without it!"

I felt happy also in the thought that at last I had something to show for the use I was making of my spare time and I hoped that it might some day lead on to something better too.

One Sunday evening in Gurthagreenane I went to an open-air concert and for the first time in my life I heard the bagpipes playing. Never in my life had I heard anything grander. I was driven half crazy by the wild spirited music swelling out into the air. Its pathos sent a thrill of fervour through my blood. I thought of Kenneth O'Hara. His handsome figure came before me in a dream of glory, leading all the kind and friendly people of Ireland in a march of splendour to the music. It was the Killarney Pipers Band. They wore a uniform of green jackets and yellow kilts, the last word in Irish national colours. I could never forget the scene as they stood on a platform under the great oak trees at the side of the sports-field opposite to the chapel for ever associated now with Father Ambrose and his Mission in my mind.

When that concert was over, my fiddles no longer satisfied me. I had such a longing for the bagpipes that I thought of them night and day. At that time I had about as much hope of getting a set of pipes as I had of sitting on the throne of England, but I said to myself, that if I could at all by honest means, I would get them. By God's grace, in the end, my desire got so strong that it became a dynamo which kept my brain working and my hands acting until, over what seemed mountains of difficulties thrown in my way, I supplied myself with them. I had often heard of what is called a dookaun, made by cutting a slit near the joint in a piece of straw. When this slit is blown into, a squeaky sound of the same tone as a bagpipe reed is produced. I had never heard but the one note produced from it, but my father had a story of Daniel O'Connell, the Liberator, coming across a young lad playing music on one of these dookauns. If that boy could do it, said I to myself, then why not I?

I cut little holes in the straw like those on a flute. When I found myself able to produce music from it, I felt I was in heaven. I now prepared a hollow bamboo cane, with holes at regular intervals as in a fife, and putting the dookaun into the end of it I soaped the joint to make it air-tight, and blew into the slit. The volume of sound was greatly increased.

"For heaven's sake," cried my mother, coming out of the room, "take yourself and your blasted old dookaun out of here! My head is in a bourawn listening to you."

It was no small satisfaction to me though that my music was now loud enough to be heard through the wall and, carrying my instruments out to the hayshed, I played away to my heart's content.

But I did not rest there. I wanted a bag to hold the reserve wind which is necessary for bagpipe-playing. I made this from a sheepskin by sewing it tightly together; keeping it soft and pliable by means of a little treacle poured into it now and again. I also made large drone-pipes out of some alder sticks which were hollow in the middle. They grew in plenty on the ditch of our haggard. Fitting them with big droning dookauns

I attached them to the bag; then fixed on the bamboo chanter. I covered the bag with a green cloth and, having decorated the pipes with ribbons, I blew into the mouthpiece.

"Inglaaw! Inglaaw!" they squealed melodiously, and tune after tune enlivened the air.

The news of the wonderful bagpipes soon spread far and wide. A jolly neighbour told his children that as the bag should always be made from the skin of a mule to give the music its proper tone, I had lost no time in going across the valley to skin an animal of that kind which had died of old age on a neighbouring farm!

As soon as I was well practised in some tunes I went to the village of Gurthagreenane one Sunday evening. It is the custom for the country fellows to gather in there on such evenings, when they walk up and down, whistling and singing until long after dark. With a few of the Coomlaegill boys around me I started to play the pipes at one end of the street and I soon had all the people marching behind me to the other.

XXIV

"The Last Glimpse of Erin"

MANY of my companions had now left for America. Maurice O'Grady, Jamesy O'Loughlin, Clarence O'Reilly and Finnawn MacNulty, my schoolmates, had all gone, as well as many others, so it looked as if my turn was near too if I wanted to get away from farming.

The scenes at the railway station were heart-rending with mothers and fathers crying as their children waved their tear-stained handkerchiefs through the windows of the train as it steamed away for the great unknown world beyond the bogs and mountains. For many people these partings would be the last. Everyone seemed to know it, for America was far away and the years were long and lonely. The last wailing whistle of the train going out of sight around the foot of the steep rocky cliffs through The Glen of the Other World was worse than the wail of a shrouded fairy woman and, after they had heard it, those who were left behind went home like mourners from a new-made grave.

Between these partings however the dances went on as usual and, while I was pondering on my coming fate, I attended one that was held in the house of O'Sullivan Corrig, near the village of Gurthagreenane. I remember the event in particular because while attending it I heard the loveliest singing that human ears could enjoy.

It was the custom at such gatherings that when the young people grew tired of dancing they would sit down and ask someone to sing. This person and that would give their verses as best they could after a lot of wearisome coaxing and persuasion. "Go on now, Shaun. Give us the song the old cow died of," or "Come on, Mary, girl. Don't let down Slievemore," and so forth. Often when the song finally came, Shaun and Mary would have had the value of their singing well out of the people by trying their patience as well as wasting their time, and then rewarding them with poor singing in the end. They had to be cautious, of course, because if their contributions did not please the audience an uneasy whispering and giggling would soon show them the way the wind was blowing, and the world knows that a smothered giggle is worse than an open laugh. On this occasion, however, when all the local singers had done their best, someone called on a young girl of about twenty who had just returned from America where she had spent some years with her uncle, and asked her for a song. She was a daughter to White-river Denny, the Fiddler from Coom. Unlike the others she kept nobody waiting but stood up at once with her back to the fire, facing everyone with the self-possession of a trained artist. That called my attention to her at once. I had never seen anyone act like that before. All the other singers had remained sitting with their heads drooping like sick chickens while drawling out their rustic verses. Helen, for that was her name, stood up as straight as a rush, and a very beautiful girl she was, with fair hair, big grey eyes, sharp features and a clear fresh complexion. When she began to sing, the bell-like tones of her glorious voice brought waves of rapture to my lonely heart. A sound of melody like it I had never heard before. Its beauty and loveliness was far greater than that of Nellie Melba whose voice I had the great pleasure of hearing on a gramophone record. I felt myself transported to the last realm of celestial bliss when Helen began, turning her dreamy eyes to heaven as if her own soul were far away among the angels and above the moon and stars:

"I'm thinking to-night of the old rustic bridge
  That bends o'er the murmuring stream;
 'Twas there, Maggie dear, with our hearts full of cheer,
 We strayed 'neath the moon's gentle gleam:
 'Twas there I first met you, the light of your eyes
 Awoke in my heart a sweet thrill:
 Tho' now far away, still my thoughts fondly stray
 To the old rustic bridge by the mill.

  Beneath it the stream gently rippled;
  Around it the birds loved to trill;
  Tho' now far away, still my thoughts fondly stray
  To the old rustic bridge by the mill."

I hardly knew where I was with the great sense of pleasure her singing gave me. She went on, swaying her body gently from side to side, keeping time as it were to the pathos of her theme while we all sat there enraptured in a dream of perfect loveliness.

My mother had heard her sing on a previous occasion at the wedding of Daniel O'Falvey at Slievelea and had come home full of enthusiasm about her singing, telling us that since she had left America long ago she had never heard anything like it. Everyone in the place agreed that her voice was unsurpassed in loveliness.

The applause she got was wonderful, of course, and why not? She was asked to sing again. Her brother, who was with her, tuned up his fiddle and played while she sang:

"Though the last glimpse of Erin with sorrow I see,
Yet wherever thou art shall seem Erin to me:
In exile thy bosom shall still be my home,
And thine eyes make my climate wherever we roam.

To the gloom of some desert or cold rocky shore,
Where the eye of the stranger shall haunt us no more,
I will fly with my colleen and think the rough wind
Less rude than the foes we leave frowning behind.

And I'll gaze on thy gold hair as graceful it wreathes,
And hang o'er thy soft harp as wildly it breathes:
Nor dread that the cold-hearted Saxon shall tear
One cord from that harp or one lock from that hair."

I had never heard anything more enchanting. It was as if a fairy songster and musician had come in from Theernanogue to entertain us. I hung my head to hide the tears that ran like rivers down my cheeks, for soon I too would be having my "last glimpse of Erin" on my way across the broad Atlantic.

When the dance was over the beautiful Helen went back to her home on the mountains and there she continued to sing where few but the goats and sheep could hear her putting shame on all the nightingales and silence on the larks.

When I had done the work on our farm a cousin of ours from The Falls of Rielanna got me to help him with his, in return for which he gave me money to buy an old bicycle, held together with wire, tin and strings. I spent my spare time repairing this for another journey to Annaweelogue, this time in daylight and with my parents' consent.

The sea was calling me and I had to go like my ancestor did long ago when his brother Curney came for him on a white horse from the other world, the Lord save us. I started off in the middle of the summer and I had a glorious journey in spite of the fact that my bicycle broke down several times. I was always able to mend it again, thank God, though sometimes I had to walk from ten to fifteen miles when something went wrong which I could not fix without a new part being had from a cycle shop. In the end, after all, I reached Annaweelogue safely and was delighted to see all my friends again.

Kenneth and I went about together as before. He took me to Dursey Island where he and I had many relatives. Here too, as on the mainland, we were treated with boundless hospitality. A rough stony bohereen connected the three villages there and led to the wild western point from which there was a magnificent view of the mighty heaving ocean beyond. Looking inland the island seemed for all the world like the back of a huge prehistoric monster sticking up out of the water.

The people on the island had some quaint superstitions. While the English Carew was laying siege to Dunboy on the mainland, some of his soldiers in Dursey amused themselves by throwing the islanders over the great black cliffs at the northern side. Since then, nobody on the island will call out to another by his or her Christian name at night for fear of being answered by the spirit of one of the victims. I suppose they think the dead are often lonely and like a conversation!

When we returned to the mainland Kenneth took me lobster-fishing in his father's boat. Some of the older men, wearing long grey beards, were with us, and they were very superstitious. Many things, according to them, should never be talked about at sea, or else the fishing would be a failure. Priests and foxes should never be even mentioned. I knew nothing of this, so the clever playboys led the conversation in such a way that if I answered their questions it was inevitable that I should mention either priest or fox. It was then the whiskery old fishermen would look at me and frown, to the great delight of

205

Kenneth and his companions holding their sides with laughter at the other end of the boat.

Poor Kenneth, being human, had his faults, of course, and was no angel in spite of his looking like one, but in my great love for him I was always ready to regard even his faults as virtues, like the mussel that covers the grit it cannot remove from inside its shell with a substance that changes it into a beautiful pearl. He was very fond of drink and wanted me to take it with him. I refused, remembering my mother's advice in the past to keep away from it because it had brought ruin to her own family as well as to many others in Ireland.

"Have a cigarette, Brian," he said, handing one to me as we stood at the cross-roads talking to his friends.

"No, thank you, Kenneth; I don't smoke," I said, for I disliked the taste and smell of tobacco, having inherited the aversion from my mother.

"You don't smoke, is it?" he said, pursing his shapely lips in sudden contempt, for he was very fond of "the weed" himself, like all his companions who had easy money from the fishing; so different from the boys of Coomlaegill who had so little in their pockets and did not smoke as a result.

"No, I don't," I said firmly, shocked at the unexpected change in his usual attitude towards me, preparing for a squall and fully determined to keep a vow I had once made never to smoke.

"Be a man," he persisted, "and have a smoke."

I looked at him and wondered how having a smoke could make a man of anyone. On the contrary, I thought, as I flared up, it took the courage of a better man to refuse if he thought fit.

But Kenneth could not see my point.

"Go on," he said, jeering at me in front of his companions who were laughing at my embarrassment as he pushed the cigarette into my mouth.

I threw it away at once, looked into his eyes and, as there was no sign of sympathy in them, I turned on my heel, pouting like a child, and walked away. He called after me but I never stopped or even looked back till I reached my Aunt Kathleen's, had my supper and went to bed.

I did not go to sleep for a long time, thinking of this most sudden change in so dear a friend. I did not see him on the following night or on the night after either, though I never stopped thinking about him. But finally I could stick the strain no longer so I went out to look for him.

"I'm sorry, Brian, if I offended you," he said when we met.

"That's all right, Kenneth," I said, soothingly, when I saw him hang his head. "I can forgive you. If it had been anyone else I wouldn't have minded so much, but you know how a small wound from a close friend hurts more than a big one from an enemy."

"I suppose you're right," he said, "but an odd cigarette with your friend does you no harm either. You're no good for making your way with others and maybe the smoking would help you."

"Maybe it would, indeed," I said with a touch of sarcasm, "and so would the drink too, for it helps many people."

"Who might they be?" he asked, knitting his brows, for he thought I was referring to himself, because I had been asking him to stop drinking whiskey after I had found him senseless from it some time previously in the village of Cluin.

"The publicans!" I said, laughing, and we left it at that.

We met again on the night before I left for home. He said he intended going to America soon and hoped to meet me there some day later on. We parted then with as much love in our hearts as when first we walked the roads together.

Dear lovely gentle Kenneth, your sweet memory stays green for ever in my mind. You stand before me always, courteous, cheerful and good-natured. Friendship keeps its early freshness and boyhood never loses beauty.

At home I am only certain of one thing with regard to my future way of living, namely, that farming is not the life for me. I am still on the sunny side of twenty, thank God. I do not want to leave Ireland of the pleasant memories but like thousands of others I will have to go because Dark Rosaleen has nothing to offer me but a spade.

Soon I shall be standing outside the house looking at the deep blue hills with the sun gone down behind them for the last time leaving a yellow glow upon the spot I love as I look back into the happy past and think of all the people I have known: the O'Mahoneys, MacNamaras, O'Kanes, O'Gradys, O'Loughlins and so forth, with Maura Nee Lhaera, Pat Mulloy and Paddy Don't Care, as well as my own people. My life in The Valley of Bright Love will then be like a book with the last page open. Soon it will be shut for ever and no man will feel like taking it in exchange for his cow, like the Golden Book of Coomlaegill, that lies unopened in a fairy mansion, for ever hidden from the sight of Man.